Looking

**Personal Memories of Uganda
1970-20**

Editor

Patricia Haward

FOUNTAIN PUBLISHERS
Kampala

Fountain Publishers
P. O. Box 488
Kampala - Uganda
E-mail: sales@fountainpublishers.co.ug
          publishing@ fountainpublishers.co.ug
Website: www.fountainpublishers.co.ug

Distributed in Europe and Commonwealth countries outside Africa by:
African Books Collective Ltd,
P. O. Box 721,
Oxford OX1 9EN, UK.
Tel/Fax: +44(0) 1869 349110
E-mail: orders@africanbookscollective.com
Website: www.africanbookscollective.com

Distributed in North America by:
Michigan State University Press
1405 South Harrison Road
25 Manly Miles Building
East Lansing, MI 48823-5245
E-mail: msupress@msu.edu
Website: www.msupress.msu.edu

© Fountain Publishers 2009
First published 2009

All rights reserved. No part of this publication may be reproduced, stored in a retrieval system or transmitted in any form or by any means electronic, mechanical, photocopying, recording or otherwise without the prior written permission of the publisher.

ISBN 978-9970-02-365-3

Contents

Foreword — v
Emmanuel Cardinal Wamala

Introduction — vii
Margaret Sekagya

Historical Context — xi
David Mukholi

1. **Detained in Nakasero** — 1
   Musekura-Rwenduru

2. **Hide and Seek in the Ministry of Information** — 7
   John Kihika

3. **The Murder of Nekemia Bananuka** — 20
   Elia-Georges Muhindi

4. **To Russia without Love** — 25
   Tumusiime-Encebebe

5. **Sucked into the Barrel** — 32
   N. Besigiroha

6. **Bomb Disposal Expert** — 41
   N. Besigiroha

7. **Dilemma in Dicey Situations 1979** — 49
   George Akol

8. **Living with Death** — 56
   Peace Anguzu

9. **Cookie Night** — 64
   T.L. Kisembo Bahemuka

10. **Panda Gari Experience** — 68
    Yosam Baguma

11. **Those Days in Luwero** — 72
    Henry Mutibwa

12. **Forced to Rape** — 77
    Godfrey Olukya

13. **Escaped Escorting a Corpse** — 81
    Roy Golooba Kalema

14. **Walking Chimney's Legacy** — 90
    Julius Ocwinyo

15. **The Last of the Jungle Foxes** — 95
    Olupot James Peter Egoing

16. **A Narrow Escape from God's Soldiers** — 103
    Oola Patrick Lumumba

17. **Bloody Hours Begin** — 111
    Davis Dickens Opira

18. **Ambush** — 116
    Oloya Okot

19. **A Hospital on the Kampala-Gulu Road** — 125
    Dr Stanley Kiwanuka Kitaka

20. **A West Nile Bandit in the City** — 129
    Yuni Mi

21. **The Dumping Grounds** — 134
    Joshua Kato

22. **An Encounter with Friendly Enemies** — 143
    Fortunate Tabaro Nkera

23. **Massacre** — 147
    JWL

24. **Terror on the Road** — 151
    Masyale Sowedi Wayenga

Foreword

The end of the rule of Obote I marked the beginning of the rule of Idi Amin which was to unleash untold woes for Ugandans and people of other races living in our country.

The publication of an anthology of personal stories covering a period of almost thirty years comes at a time when Ugandans are striving to reconstruct their country in physical, moral and social terms.

The expulsion of Israelis and people of Asian origin was the first blow that Amin inflicted on our society. Not only did it hurt the victims for whom it was intended, but also perhaps even more the Ugandans who, in the mind of our nation's leader, were supposed to gain. From that time Uganda's economy started its downward descent, which continues to the present day.

The disappearance of the Chief Justice, Benedict Kiwanuka, the first Ugandan in that high office; the murder of the Governor of the Bank of Uganda, Joseph Mubiru, again the first Ugandan in that office; the abduction of Msgr Clement Mukasa from the altar and his subsequent disappearance, also that of Byron Kawaddwa from the National Theatre; the murder of Mr Kawalya and that of Fr Clement Kiggundu, both of whom were charred beyond recognition; the shooting of Mrs Bukenya Nanziri at Makerere; and the murder of Archbishop Luwum together with three ministers; these and other similar horrors became the order of the day during Amin's eight years of rule of terror. They proved to Ugandans that the situation was unprecedented and unparalleled and that the country was heading for total destruction.

The collection of the present stories, as we could expect, is a selection out of many which have not found space in this anthology. Moreover, they are stories of those fortunate ones who survived the murderous regimes and can tell their experience. But we can stretch our imagination to the experiences of the hundreds who never lived to narrate their ordeal. They were bundled and locked up in boots, whisked away to places of torture and we never knew how they ended their earthly lives!

In June 1978 Christians in Uganda opened the celebration of the centenary of faith. On 3rd June pilgrims from Tanzania informed us that the Wakombozi, the Liberators, were preparing to come. The news was too good to be true. When they arrived at the beginning of 1979 who among true lovers of humankind and of our country would not welcome them? The overthrow of Amin was welcomed in Uganda, in the neighbouring countries and beyond.

To most Ugandans the return of Obote engineered by fellow Ugandans and backed by Tanzania was nothing but betrayal. Obote II regime did not continue from where Obote had stopped in 1971, it continued from where Amin had stopped. It continued with a spirit of hatred and revenge. This time it was not a matter of arbitrary arrest and imprisonment, it meant destruction of villages quite close to genocide. To the present day human skulls, relics of the years 1981 to 1985, can still be seen in various parts of Luweero Triangle. Some Ugandans who went into exile during this time of Obote II and during the previous years have not yet had the courage to return to their country.

The stories narrating experiences during the last 14 years may have some echoes of misery but those of the future will surely sound different. Please God, may they signal the end of Uganda's woes.

+Emmanuel Cardinal Wamala
Archbishop of Kampala

Introduction

Margaret Sekaggya
Chairperson, Uganda Human Rights Commission

Most countries of the world have had their ugly, bad and traumatising past. They have had histories of dictatorship and human rights violations. In the African continent there are those leaders who, it was said, were even cannibals. Others have had their citizens subjected to most of the crimes against humanity including genocide, mutilation and many other horrible experiences. From Germany to Rwanda and from Uganda to Sierra Leone, many other countries have their own particular stories to tell. However, the international community does not judge our situations on the basis of how much we agonise over our bad history alone. We shall be judged on what we have done to put our bad history right. Our resolute determination to put our history back on course and move forward to join the civilised world of peace, reconciliation, reconstruction, democracy, good governance, constitutionalism and the rule of law, will enable us to forget the horrendous experiences of the past. Since 1986, the people of Uganda seem to have said "never again to the bad past" where state barbarism, state terrorism and widespread violation of human rights were the order of the day.

Violation of human rights was the *raison d'etre* for the "bush war". The experiences in this book are only the tip of the iceberg. There are more experiences documented in the Report of the Commission of Inquiry into Human Rights Violations from 1962-85. Government set up this commission that was headed by Justice Arthur Oder only four months after it captured power in 1986. This was only one of the first steps that demonstrated that the state was determined to put a halt to the senseless violations of human rights. The commission was mandated to investigate violations of human rights from 9 October 1962 (when Uganda got its independence) to the time the National Resistance Army/Movement (NRA/M) took over on 16 January 1986. This commission inquired into all aspects of violations of human rights, breaches of the rule of law and the excessive abuses of power committed against persons in Uganda by the regimes in power, their servants, agents or agencies, by whatever name called, and was mandated to "find possible ways of preventing the re-occurrence of the aforesaid matters".

The 1500-page report of the commission exposes the extent of the ruthlessness of the past regimes. The experiences in this book, *Looking Back,* are added testimony to the brutality and the consequences of bad governance. The experiences in this book do not only show the extent of the violations but also depict the struggles and sacrifices of most people in Uganda under the brutal regimes of the past. They clearly demonstrate that states can kill their citizens, and also that they cannot eliminate all of them nor can they break the resilience and stamina of the people and their determiantion to continue struggling. In fact the more brutal and tyrannical the regimes became, the more the people became aware of what they were lacking in terms of human rights and democracy.

This book brings out glaring cases of torture. States tend to use torture as a method of extracting evidence from suspects. This is one of the most primitive methods which, unfortunately, is still used in most states. It is a method that should be rejected, condemned and abandoned altogether by state agents. The major criticism of this method is that it usually penalises the innocent. The case of Musekura -Rwenduru in "Detained in Nakasero" in this book is a good example of torturing an innocent victim. Arbitrary arrests, frogmarching, detentions without trial, disposal of corposes in forests, rivers, etc and violations of the rights of suspects that are unheard of in civilised societies are what Masekura – Rwenduru reminds us of.

1986 to-date (2001) has seen a process of institutional transformation through broad consultation, participation and debate, creation of human rights awareness, constitution-making and the consolidation of good governance. This period witnessed the formation of the Commission of Inquiry into Violations of Human Rights (1986-95), of the Uganda Constitutional Commission headed by Justice Benjamin Odoki (1989-93), the Constituent Assembly elections and politics (1994-95) and the promulgation of the new constitution in 1995. The inclusion of the Bill of Rights in Chapter Four of the constitution where human rights are enshrined, including the rights of persons with disabilities and other marginalized groups, and the establishment of the Uganda Human Rights Commission, are some of the landmarks of the struggles of the people of Uganda. The experiences of Godfrey Olukya in "Forced Rape" in this book would probably never have taken place or gone unpunished if the existing institutions such as the UHRC, an independent judiciary, a sensitised populace and a vibrant civil society of women and PWDs that we have today had been in place.

The book also brings to mind memories of 'refugeeism' and internal displacement. State-inspired violence creates insecurity. Those who are not lucky to run away and become refugees lose their lives or become internally displaced persons. Indeed the number of people who lost their lives was greater than that of those who became refugees. Those who became refugees like Tumusiime Encebebe in "To Russia With Love" are lucky to be alive and tell their story, but such stories should form a basis of determination on our part to put a stop to the creation of conditions that lead to the exodus of our people from our country.

Currently the major challenge we have is the problem of internally displaced persons (IDPs). Over 180, 000 persons are IDPs. Internal displacement of persons has been brought about by the insurgences in some parts of western and northern Uganda. In these places insecurity has stagnated development in all sectors. This is why the story of Olupot James Peter Egoing, "The Last of the Jungle Foxes", is essential for people to realise that there can be reconstruction after destruction. The ending of rebellion in eastern Uganda (Soroti) and the development that has accrued from the reconstruction process are a good lesson for the people in the currently disturbed areas to emulate. The peasants, the children, the women, the IDPs and PWDs who are the innocent victims of senseless warfare want peace, as Egoing testifies, "to look after their chickens", and all peace-loving Ugandans should utilise the conducive environment to resolve whatever conflicts they have amicably using the existing legal institutions. Since we now have them, we should and can maintain and utilise them.

The Uganda Human Rights Commission (UHRC), using its constitutional mandate to, among other things, investigate and handle complaints of human rights, will do all in its power to contribute towards human rights promotion and protection. We have an obligation to sensitise the population about the constitution and other human rights instruments. We have the powers of the courts and we can demand any remedies, including compensation, for whatever human rights are violated. The functions of UHRC are clearly stated in articles 52 and 53 of the constitution. Together we can build a better Uganda.

The way forward is for Ugandans to cultivate a culture of valuing constitutionalism, the rule of law and good governance among themselves. The promotion and protection of human rights should result from the concerted efforts of all Ugandans. Let us all ensure that Uganda does not return to the ugly past. Let all Ugandans promote and preserve peace.

Historical Context
David Mukholi

Since independence, Uganda's history is dominated by misrule, violation of human rights, breakdown of law and order and economic decline. A chequered era. Testimonies presented in this book accentuate extreme brutality, demeaning humanity and mocking independence expectations.

When Uganda gained independence on 9th October 1962, the people celebrated in anticipation of a bright future. But soon independent Uganda slipped into tyranny, anarchy, dictatorship and war. The promised rule of law, respect of human rights and democracy faded into extra-judicial killings, detention without trial, arrogance and intolerance by oppressive regimes.

Dr Apollo Milton Obote took the reins of the newly independent country as Executive Prime Minister following an alliance between Uganda People's Congress (UPC) and Kabaka Yekka (KY) a Buganda tribal party. In 1963 the National Assembly elected Sir Edward Mutesa, the Kabaka of Buganda, as a ceremonial president of Uganda with the Kyabazinga of Busoga, Sir William Wilberforce Nadiope as Vice President.

UPC/KY alliance did not stand the test of time as a power struggle between Obote and Mutesa ensued. Obote emerged winner, overthrowing Mutesa by abrogating the constitution in the most foul and undemocratic manner. Obote named himself president.

Buganda, irked by Obote's move reacted by ordering the Uganda government to vacate Buganda. This triggered the 1966 crisis. Obote responded with force. He ordered the army under the command of the Deputy Army Commander Col. Idi Amin to attack the Kabaka's Palace (Lubiri). Many lives and much property were lost in the raid. But Mutesa managed to escape into exile in Britain where he lived and eventually died in 1969.

A state of emergency was declared in Buganda. This robbed the Baganda of their freedom. Gatherings were proscribed, possession of any item that identified Buganda kingdom was a crime. Government used the emergency powers to arrest and detain anyone opposed to it.

Rule under independent Uganda became more repressive than the colonial era. The government between 1966 and 1970 was largely a civilian dictatorship protected by the army.

The government lacked the electoral mandate to rule but Obote carved out loyal officers in the army to ensure his continued unlawful stay in power.

In December 1969, the state of emergency was extended to the rest of the country following the attempted assassination of Obote. All political organisations were banned except UPC and Uganda henceforth became a one-party state.

The politics of intrigue and manipulation spewed tribalism in government, including the security forces. By 1970, Obote's power base in the army was crumbling. The army was intractably divided along tribes. Amin had managed to recruit a big following of West Nilers and other Sudanic tribes. And Obote was pushing his Acholi and Langi favourites up the army hierarchy. He also created a personal army, the General Safety Unit (GSU) under the command of his cousin, Akena Adoko.

This set the stage for a final showdown between Obote and Amin.

Amin publicly complained about the political situation in the country. Corruption, disunity, robbery were widespread. Ugandans had no freedom. Amin advised Obote to hold elections in 1971. To Obote this was tantamount to insubordination but he feared to arrest Amin because of the big following he had in the army. Relations between the two deteriorated as both struggled to gain control over the army.

Amin was suspected to have participated in the attempted assassination of Obote. He was also implicated in the murder of Brigadier Okoya and his wife in Gulu in January 1970. Obote was grooming Okoya, an Acholi, to replace Amin as Army Commander.

There were numerous rumours about coup plots as Obote and Amin struggled to outdo one another.

Obote managed to gain a temporary upperhand in September 1970 when he effected changes in the army, sidelining Amin. Brigadier Hussein was appointed Chief of Staff (effectively becoming the army's commander) and Col. Juma was made Chief of Air Force. Amin's new position, Chief of Defence Forces, was more of a figurehead.

Before he left for Singapore, in January 1971, to attend the Commonwealth summit, Obote summoned Amin and showed him two reports. One was the Auditor General's about overspending in the army without authority. And the other was about the murder of Brig. Okoya.

When Obote flew to Singapore on January 13th he left behind a memo to Amin to explain the two issues. Amin was accused of failing to account for the army expenditure and killing Okoya. Obote also left instructions to a special committee to arrest Amin. The committee comprised of the Minister of Internal Affairs, Basil Bataringaya; Inspector General of Police, Erinayo Oryema; the Chief of Staff Brigadier Hussein and Lt. Col. Oyite-Ojok the Quartermaster, army headquarters.

Amin survived the arrest by seizing power and plunged the country into deep political, social and economic troubles.

On January 25th 1971, Amin took over government. He told the country that he was a simple professional soldier and not a politician. And he defended the coup as a means to save the country from bloodshed and economic collapse.

Amin gave 18 reasons to justify the overthrow of Obote:
1. Unwarranted detention of people without trial.
2. Continuation of the state of emergency.
3. Lack of freedom to air political views.
4. The frequent loss of life and property from armed robberies.
5. The proposals for National Service.
6. Widespread corruption in high places especially ministers and civil servants.
7. The failure by political authorities to organise any elections and the proposed three-plus-one electoral method which would favour the rich.
8. Economic policies that had caused poverty and unemployment.
9. High taxes, e.g. Development, Graduated, Sales and Social Security Fund.
10. Low prices for crops as opposed to high cost of food and education.

11. Isolating Uganda from East Africa by sending away Kenyans and refusing Kenya and Tanzania currencies in Uganda.
12. The creation of a wealthy class of leaders.
13. Failure of the Defence Council to meet under its chairman the President.
14. Training of a second army of people from Akokoro county where Obote and Akena Adoko come from.
15. The Lango Development Master Plan which was designed to give all key position in politics, army and commercial/individual sector to people from Akokoro in Lango.
16. Dividing the army and giving Langi top positions.
17. Using the cabinet office to down grade and divide the army through robbery.
18. All the matters mentioned were leading to bloodshed.

Amin's coup was received with enthusiasm and excitement especially in Buganda. Thousands of Ugandans poured into the streets in jubilation at the fall of Obote. Amin's action marked the end of misrule under Obote and UPC in many people's minds.

To many Ugandans, Amin was a saviour, rescuing the country from the wrath of Obote's dictatorship. They expected Amin to end tyranny, oppression, corruption, and tribalism afflicting the country.

But the jubilations and cheers that ushered in the military regime soon turned into despair, desolation and death. The overthrow of Obote underlined transition from one dictatorship to another.

Two years after the coup, Amin's 18 points were in ridicule. Terror returned. State inspired killings, misconduct by the armed forces and mismanagement of the economy deflated the spirit of Ugandans. A brutal reign of terror had begun.

A wave of killings following the coup was a precursor to doom. Amin started eliminating opposition within the army by systematically killing all soldiers of Acholi and Langi origin. From 1971-1972 hundreds of them were massacred. Soldiers suspected of being loyal to the ousted regime were also murdered.

Killings spread to the civilian population. Supporters of UPC and Obote were targeted. The military regime did not spare civil servants and intellectuals, fearing that they would mobilise the opposition against it.

Many people arrested were killed and dumped in Namanve and Mabira forests. Others were thrown into the River Nile. It was common to see floating bodies on the Nile. Several people had to flee the country before the brutal regime caught up with them (Ref. 4. "To Russia Without Love by Tumusiime-Encebebe).

The lucky ones were arrested, tortured and released. But some of those arrested disappeared without trace to date. While others were detained in uninhabitable dungeons and left to die there. At the collapse of Amin's government several Ugandans were rescued from the State Research Bureau torture and death chambers in Nakasero, Kampala. (Ref. 1. "Detained in Nakasero" by Musekura-Rwenduru)

Among prominent civilians who disappeared without trace were Benedicto Kiwanuka, former DP leader and the Chief Justice; Joseph Mubiru; Governor of the Bank of Uganda; and Frank Kalimuzo, the Vice-Chancellor of Makerere University.

Tribal killings depleted the ranks of the armed forces. Amin had to recruit from among the former Anyanya (Nubian) fighters of Southern Sudan and Simba rebels from eastern Zaire (now Democratic Republic of Congo).

The tribal balance in the army shifted from dominance of Acholi and Langi to West Nilers including the Alur, Bari, Kakwa and Lugbara.

Amin also preferred uneducated ruthless soldiers who did not question his political authority and actions. Civilians lived in fear. No one dared stand up against army men (Ref. "14. Walking Chimney's Legacy" by Julius Ocwinyo). Uneducated soldier easily accepted the brutal responsibility to purge any resistance and eliminate opponents of the regime. They would kill and ask questions after. Lack of education instilled inferiority complex in a large section of the army buttressing brutality (Ref. "5. Sucked into the Barrel" and Ref. "6. Bomb Disposal Expert" both by B. Besigiroha).

The army and other security agencies like the State Research Bureau (SRB), Public Safety Unity (PSU) and the Anti-Smuggling Unit (ASU) were staffed with Amin loyalists and had licence to kill. They were above the law.

Such enormous powers allowed gross indiscipline in the forces. Sometimes it was to settle personal scores. And often security personnel were also available to any civilian who wanted to eliminate another. Some civilians took advantage of the situation to falsely implicate others to settle pretty rivalry in villages or work places (Ref. "7. Living with Death" by George Akol).

Women particularly suffered the heaviest brunt of the regime's high handedness. Soldiers had unquestionable powers to grab any women and forcefully marry them. A woman who dared resist would be killed. Rape by army men was rampant.

It was common for a soldier to pick on any woman even the married one. Amin himself had set an example by killing Sarah Kyolaba's fiance and taking her on as his wife.

In September 1972, an invasion from Tanzania by Ugandans in exile to overthrow Amin was crushed. The ill trained invaders were beaten off and several captured. Those captured and suspected sympathisers were publicly executed in their districts of origin. Amin's security agents also combed western Uganda in search of the coordinators and collaborators of the invasion. Those arrested were killed on the spot (Ref. "3. The Murder of Nekemia Bananuka" by Elia-Georges Mulindi).

Several coup and assassination attempts on Amin provoked fierce reprisal on innocent civilians. In 1974, two coup plots were foiled. One in February led by Lt. Col. Michael Ondoga and another in March by Brig. Charles Arube.

As the political order disintegrated, the economy collapsed. In 1972 Amin launched the 'economic war' and expelled all Asians from Uganda. All their properties were confiscated and allocated to Ugandans who lacked entrepreneurial skills. Industrial and business establishments crumbled in rot. There was severe shortage of essential commodities. Inflation spiralled to hyper levels and the economy declined. There was no crop finance to pay farmers for their cash crops. This led to speculation, hoarding, smuggling and black-marketing locally known as *Magendo*.

Magendo business was risky. Often traders were arrested and shot on the spot accused of being saboteurs. But this did not stop several Ugandans risking their lives to earn a living through Magendo. Frustration and hopelessness compelled many to join. Magendo was entrenched to the extent that it lived on long after the fall of Idi Amin in 1979. So did the brutality to crush the illicit trade (Ref. "22. An Encounter with Friendly Enemies" by Fortunate Tabaro Nkera).

Every aspect of life was distorted during Amin's era. Not only did Ugandans have to succumb to scarcities but also to repressive policies. For instance mini dresses, wigs and make up were outlawed. Any woman found wearing them was arrested and publicly caned.

Makerere University glowed with feeble resistance, but it also soon bowed to the brutal regime. In 1976 Amin sent troops to quell a student demonstration in response to the killing of a student by the army. Soldiers went on a looting, torturing and raping spree at the campus.

When Christian churches attempted to speak out against human rights violation, they became the next victims. Twenty-six Christian organisations were banned leaving the Protestant and Catholic churches only.

The persecution of Christians reached its peak with the murder of the Archbishop of the Church of Uganda, Janani Luwum, in 1977. The Protestant prelate was killed along side two minister, Lt. Col. Erinayo Oryema and Charles Oboth Ofumbi, on accusations of being in contact with Obote in a plot to overthrow Amin.

By the end of Amin's reign in 1979 an estimated 500,000 Ugandans had been killed. Amin had sown seeds of fear, discord, discrimination that were to linger on into the future (Ref. "2. Hide and Seek in the Ministry of Information" by John Kihika)

From the time Amin took power in 1971, Tanzanian President Julius Nyerere, who was a personal friend of Obote, refused to recognise him as president of Uganda. He generously granted asylum to several Ugandans fleeing Amin's brutal regime.

In 1978, Amin committed a costly blunder - invading Tanzania and annexing the Kagera Salient. The provocative act led to his downfall. The Tanzania Peoples Defence Force (TPDF) fought back creating an opportunity for Ugandans in exile to join the liberation of war after years of preparation. Amin's retreating soldiers looted, raped and killed several civilians (Ref. "24. Terror on the Road" by Musyate Sowedi Wayenga, Ref. "7. Dilemma in Dicey Situations" by George Akol)

Ugandan fighters operated under the umbrella of the Uganda National Liberation Army (UNLA). The two main groups in the UNLA were Front for National Salvation (FRONASA) led by Yoweri Museveni and Obote's force, *Kikosi Maalum,* commanded by Tito Okello and David Oyite-Ojok.

Amin's reign of terror ended on April 11, 1979. A transitional government under Uganda National Liberation Front (UNLF) was installed with Prof. Yusuf Lule as President.

UNLF comprised of all political and armed groups that had participated in the war against Amin. Its internal organs included the National Consultative Council (NCC) and the National Executive Committee (NEC) as the supreme organ and executive arm respectively. The former, under the chairmanship of Prof. Edward Rugumayo and the latter was headed by Yusuf Lule.

Other organs included the Military Commission chaired by Paulo Muwanga with Yoweri Museveni a Vice Chairman. The Political and Diplomatic Commission was headed by Prof. Dan Wadada Nabudere and Finance and Administration was under Semei Nyanzi.

Once again Ugandans excitedly welcomed the new government. After years of state inspired terror and economic decline, the obsession to celebrate was overriding. But it was also short lived. Divergent political interests and opinions triggered power struggles in the UNLF. Lule was deposed within 68 days.

The removal of Lule prompted demonstrations in Kampala under the banner NO LULE NO WORK. The army had to be called in to disperse the demonstrators.

Uganda remained a divided country even after the fall of Amin. All organs of UNLF were smeared by politics of conflicts, intrigue and manipulation.

UNLA was dominated by pro-Obote and UPC soldiers with only a small fraction inclined to Museveni. And Tanzanian troops came out openly as power brokers favouring Obote.

Lule was replaced by Godfrey Binaisa. But the change did not salvage the country from insecurity and violence perpetrated by UNLA.

UNLA was equally as indisciplined as Amin's army. They hunted for former soldiers and anyone closely associated with Amin's regime and killed them. West Nile, home of Amin, was devastated by killing and looting. Nearly the entire population fled to Sudan and Zaire (Democratic Republic of Congo) (Ref. "20. West Nile Bandit in the City" by Yuni Mi).

Smuggling, hoarding and scarcities persisted. (Ref."22. An Encounter with Friendly Enemies" by Foruntate Tabaro Nkera). The new political leaders started using their position to acquire wealth justifying it to their contribution to the liberation of Uganda. But it was a mock liberation and Ugandans continued to suffer under the liberators.

Binaisa attempted to consolidate power, effecting changes in the UNLA government by weeding out political rivals. This ambitious move failed.

He demoted Ateker Ejalu from regional cooperation minister to an ambassadorial post. Museveni was shifted from the powerful defence ministry to regional cooperation. And Paulo Muwanga was removed from internal affairs and posted as an ambassador.

Binaisa went on to canvass support and announced elections would be held under the UNLF umbrella where all parties belonged. But UPC and DP denounced the move. His final gamble was relieving the UNLA Chief of Staff Brig. Oyite-Ojok of his duties and appointing him ambassador to Algeria.

Oyite-Ojok turned down the new post, accusing Binaisa of interfering in the running of the army. A conflict between UNLA and UNLF emerged. In the ensuing disagreement the military commission took power in May 1980 and put Binaisa under house arrest. The Military Commission under Muwanga's chairmanship went on to organise the controversial 1980 elections.

Intimidation, bribery, violence and rigging marred the elections. Muwanga himself took charge of announcing the results. The final results did not reflect the popular view – DP's victory. UPC led by Obote had 74 seats; DP headed by Paul Ssemogerere won 51. While the Uganda Patriotic Movement (UPM) got 1 seat and the Conservative Party (CP) nil led by Museveni and Mayanja Nkangi respectively.

Obote was declared the winner and sworn in as president. This opened up a new wave of oppression. Members of the opposition parties were hunted arrested and detained, some were killed (Ref. "10. Panda Gari Experience" by Yosam Baguma).

Museveni had earlier warned that if elections were rigged he would go to the bush. In February 198, Museveni with 26 men, launched a war against the Obote II regime, attacking Kabamba Military Training School.

Museveni's group – the Popular Resistance Army (PRA) later merged with Yusuf Lule's Uganda Freedom Fighters (UFF) to form the National Resistance Movement (NRM) with the National Resistance Army (NRA) as the armed wing. NRA strategically based itself in Luwero triangle near Kampala to fight Obote's government.

Other fighting groups included Uganda Freedom Movement (UFM), Uganda National Rescue Front (UNRF), Former Uganda National Army (FUNA) and the Federal Democratic Movement of Uganda (FEDEMU).

Government responded to the armed rebellion with ruthlessness and intolerance. Innocent civilians in rebel operation zones were butchered on mere suspicion, children and women were not spared. An estimated 300,000 people lost their lives at the hands of the dreaded UNLA.

The discipline in the army snapped as the rebels intensified their attacks on government troops. Soldiers terrorised the civilian population, torturing, raping and looting. Civilians, especially men were rounded up and killed. The Luwero triangle was turned into killing fields.

Families were separated as they fled the marauding UNLA troops. The soldiers captured young girls and women and turned them into wives or sex slaves (Ref. "12. Forced to Rape" by Godfrey Olukya).

Thousands of people in Luwero including women and children were massacred, houses bombed and property looted. This, however, was not limited to Luwero only other parts of the country were also under UNLA brutality. People reacted differently to the harassment. In some case they were compelled to begin plotting against the government forces (Ref. "23. Massacre" by JWL).

Luwero survivors have heart rending stories of gruesome murders, harassment and fear. Some people, especially UPC functionaries took advantage of the lawlessness to settle personal scores. Those believed to be opposed to UPC were branded as bandits and reported to the UNLA. As expected they would be arrested and sometimes killed. It was yet another opportunity when Ugandans took to settling personal conflicts by framing each other as bandits. Often jealousies and petty, rivalry led Ugandans to be labelled enemies of the state (Ref. "9. Cookie Night" by T.L. Kisembo Bahemuka).

Security organs like the Special Force and the National Security Agency (NASA) were specifically created to deal with suspected government opponents. They organised mass arrests commonly known as *Panda Gari* in various parts of the country especially in Kampala. (Ref. "13. Escaped Escorting a Corpse"). by Roy Golooba Kalema). Those arrested were thoroughly beaten and some killed. Several were incarcerated in uninhabitable cells. Women and schools girls were abducted and turned into wives (Ref. "11. Those Days in Luwero" by Henry Mutibwa). Among the most feared torture and death chambers were Nile Mansion (Serena Hotel), Argentina House, Bugolobi, Kireka barracks, Makindye barracks, NASA Headquarters Nakasero and Naguru Police barracks. Those killed were dumped in forests like Namanve and Mabira near Kampala (Ref. "21. The Dumping Grounds" by Joshua Kato).

Obote rekindled the 1960 tribal divisions in the UPC and UNLA. He embarked on building a tribal alliance in the army, favouring the Langi.

Following the death of Brig. David Oyite-Ojok, the chief of staff, in a mysterious helicopter crash in 1983 in Luwero, tribal contest in the army escalated. Senior Acholi officers were irked by Obote's appointment of Brigadier Smith Apon Acak, a Lango, to replace Oyite-Ojok. They openly resisted it. Divisions in the UNLA eventually lead to the collapse of the Obote II regime.

The Acholi faction in UNLA led by Maj. General Tito Okello and Maj. General Bazillio Okello toppled Obote on July 27th 1985. But the coup did not end the mayhem and bloodshed, security forces continued killing and robbing civilians. Many were killed during the take over. UPC supporters became the next victims of brutality.

Uganda was in turmoil. Soldiers turned into beasts. It was safer for the people to live in wild forests than in their homes.

Rebel groups including FUNA, UNRF, UFM and FEDEMU, but excepting NRA/M, heeded the military junta's call to form a national unity government. DP and a faction of UPC led by Paulo Muwanga (former Vice-President and Minister of Defence in Obote II regime) also joined Okello's government.

NRA/M refused to join the government until a political settlement was negotiated.

The sudden mix of fighting forces in government and the army plunged the country into deeper chaos and anarchy. Each fighting force had its own political agenda and score to settle.

Insecurity heightened. Kampala City was divided into military spheres of influence between various armed factions. The five months era of the military junta had the worst human rights record. Armed forces were at loose killing and looting in broad daylight.

The military junta and NRA/M finally embarked on peace talks (commonly referred to as peace jokes) between August and December 1985. Although an agreement was signed on December 17th, the war continued unabated until the NRA captured power on January 26th 1986.

Museveni took power and announced that his takeover was not 'a mere change of guards but a fundamental change'.

The UNLA (Okello forces) and their allies (mainly FUNA) looted, killed, raped and abducted civilians as they fled Kampala. (Ref. "19. A Hospital on the Kampala-Gulu Road" by Dr Stanley Kiwanuka Kitaka).

The retreating armies assembled in the north and in southern Sudan and reorganised to fight the new regime. This ushered in a new angle of insecurity.

Soon armed groups emerged to fight the NRM government. Northern and north eastern Uganda had been to some extent spared the brunt of the Obote II and Okello regimes, because the majority of UNLA and other security forces personnel were from these regions.

The new regime in Kampala immediately met resistance in northern Uganda. On 20th August 1986 a rebel force attacked Gulu town from Sudan. Lt. Gen. Bazillio Okello commanded the group calling itself Uganda People's Democratic Movement/Army (UPDM/A).

As the NRA was battling the rebels in the north, Karimojong cattle rustlers took advantage of the security laxity to invade their neighbours.

NRA managed to beat off the UPDM/A attack. The defeated rebel soldiers scattered throughout northern Uganda, committing atrocities against civilians. By the end of 1986, UPDM/A had disintegrated and collapsed. But its soldiers were to be drafted into other rebel groups.

Led by Peter Otai a former minister in Obote II regime, the Uganda Peoples Army (UPA) mostly comprised of the former dreaded Special Forces (Ref. "15. The Last of the Jungle Foxes" by Olupot James Peter Egoing) was formed. Apparently armies and security agencies that had committed crimes against humanity were fighting to regain control of government.

The NRM government unlike Obote II tried to talk to the rebels. Talks led to the end of insurgency in Teso. Government signed a peace agreement with the UPA rebels. Another peace accord with UPDM/A was also endorsed.

Government also extended amnesty and a presidential pardon to all rebels in 1987-1988. This had a temporary effect but soon new rebel groups emerged. In 1999 again, an amnesty law granting pardon to rebels was enacted.

A new rebel movement, the Holy Spirit Movement led by Alice Auma Lakwena was fomed. When it failed, another spiritually oriented group, the Lords Resistance Army (LRA) led by Joseph Kony, surfaced. LRA hadbases in southern Sudan and it was backed by the Sudan government. Government efforts to have talks with the rebels proved futile.

LRA has brutalised the civilian population of northern Uganda. The rebels mostly target civilians, cutting off their lips and limbs. Killing and abductions are LRA's main operation objective. Among the abductees are women and children. (Ref. "16. A Narrow Escape From God's Soldiers" by Oola Patrick Lumumba). For instance, in October 1996 LRA abducted 139 school girls of St. Mary's College, Aboke in Apac. Only one hundred and nine were released upon pleas from the Headmistress.

The abducted are initiated into rebel ranks by being made to kill and to drink human blood. Apart from abductions, LRA lays ambush along major roads to the north targeting civilian vehicles, killing hundreds (Ref. "18. Ambush" by Oloya Okot).

Although the NRM regime has largely transformed the economic and political order in the country, rebel activities remain a pain.

In October 1996 another rebel group started operating in western Uganda areas. The Allied Democratic Force (ADF) like the LRA targeted the civilian population.

Sometimes in its campaign against the rebels, the Uganda Peoples' Defence Force (UPDF) formerly NRA also violates human rights. But unlike previous armies, UPDF has a strict code that prescribes stiff punishment including firing squad for errant soldiers.

The NRM/A fought dictatorship to end civil strife in Uganda. But wars have continued to plague the country. This however has not frustrated the programme of restoring the rule of law, respect of human rights, democracy and managing economic recovery.

1
Detained in Nakasero

Musekura-Rwenduru

I am grateful to all those who cherish freedom, alive and dead, who have fought in various capacities to remove one of the most atrocious regimes of the present century, Idi Amin's regime.

I am one of a few surviving Ugandans who were detained for eight days in Nakasero State Research Bureau's underground cells. I regained freedom to live again on 11th April 1979, when Amin's diabolical machinery was smashed by the combined Ugandan Liberation Forces and their Tanzanian allies.

I was arrested on 3rd April 1979, during the war of liberation, at former Bokasa Street, Luwum Street today. At the time of my arrest, liberators were bombing Kampala City from Budo area, Mpigi. Reason for arrest? I hailed from western Uganda and was thus suspected to be a guerrilla.

I left Makerere University premises at around 11.00 am, and had gone to the city, together with a friend E. Tumwebaze ASP, by then an employee of Uganda Posts and Telecommunications.

Tumwebaze (still in police) had at the time taken refuge at the university campus. Most people at the time had the false belief that Makerere was one of the safest havens in Kampala.

I agreed to accompany Tumwebaze to the Post Office in the city centre, to draw money from his savings account, which he desperately needed for survival. I knew it was not safe that time to move in town but I could not shy away from him as we hailed from the same locality in Kabale.

We were stopped at Bokasa street by Amin's security men in plain clothes and others in military uniform. We were branded guerrillas on the spot. They demanded for our identity cards. I presented mine, showing that I entered Makerere University in 1976. To them that was the year I left college to train as a guerrilla in Tanzania.

The second snap question put to us was *'Kabira gani?'* literally meaning, what is your nationality (tribe)? We identified ourselves as

1

Bakiga, which to them was enough evidence that we were guerrillas. We were whipped on the street, bundled into a combi van, whisked off to the headquarters of the State Research Bureau, Nakasero.

As we were being driven to Amin's slaughter house, I asked Tumwebaze where we were being taken. When he said he thought we were headed for Nakasero, I knew I was as good as dead, for I had heard gruesome stories about the dreadful death chambers. I had spent three years in Kampala, without knowing where Nakasero was. When we approached the gates of hell, my nerves were prepared for every human being's terminal journey - death. I had one major fear. After being killed, our remains were not going to be traced by our parents and relatives.

Another dose of heavy whipping was administered to us at the gates of Nakasero. We were frog-marched to a small store (waiting room) near the main gate, where our pockets were searched, personal belongings like money and handkerchiefs, belts and shoes removed. After about thirty minutes, we were taken to the basement cells.

For the first three days we were locked in the underground front compartment, where one could see the outside world and breathe some fresh air. We were about twenty detainees in a cell that should have accommodated three to five. The number continued swelling until we were pushed into the inner, darker compartment. By that time there must have been at least fifty of us.

The first night in prison, I never ate or drank anything. The second day and third day, I drank a half litre of water, which I declined thirty six hours earlier, on account of its being dirty. I had naively hoped that we would be provided with food like any other prisoners. The remaining five days we survived on our urine. Others were forced to feed on decomposing corpses. The place was extremely humid. Some of our comrades suffocated to death. Others, obviously brought to the cells before us, had starved to death. Most of us, on seeing Amin's guards would cry: 'Saidiya maji muzeeyi' (Some water please sir).

The first five days, when we still had some semblance of strength, we were subjected to cleaning and washing the floor of the front offices, covered with pools of blood. We would use the blankets and clothes of murdered people as mops.

At times we would be called out to offload bodies of soldiers collected from the battle field. We would also load corpses of comrades who had starved to death in our cells. As the battle of Kampala became hot, there was no time to even organise for the disposal of the dead. We lived with them.

Paradoxically, we used to fight amongst ourselves in the cell. It was the law of the survival of the fittest at its worst. We fought for room where to sit and rest our aching ribs and backs. We were like too many grasshoppers locked in a calabash and exposed to glowing charcoal.

Some prisoners were averse to others making noise, perhaps in the far fetched hope that some mercy would be extended to us. Noisemakers in prison were fought by the self-appointed caretakers of discipline.

Many of us who were detained in Nakasero had literally lost hope of living again. Those who believe in the life of hereafter began preparing for the spiritual kingdom, saying their prayers. A few others protested, calling prayer another form of noise.

Many of us, once underground, were not subjected to constant beatings but left to starve to death. Three men among our group were taken for slaughter in the upper storeyed compartments where the SBR boys had refined instruments of torture.

We would only hear faint and wild noises of sometimes innocent Ugandans being tortured to death. A few of the prisoners still alive on the night of 10th April 1979 were shot by the fleeing Amin's security operatives.

Torture in the cells was not a preserve of civilians. Soldiers who were suspected of being sympathetic to the guerrillas and others caught deserting the battle front, were either brought in the cells dead, beaten to death in the front cell or forced to drink poison.

On the sixth day in prison, without food and with little water (urine) in my body, I lost sense of time. My senses of speech and hearing were also getting impaired. Up to now, I am not a fluent speaker, yet I was before incarceration. Whenever other detainees talked, I could only hear faint whispers.

Having been in a state of semi-consciousness for two days before liberation on 11th April, I cannot recall exactly how I was set free.

What I dimly remember is that during the night of 10th April, Kampala fell to the liberation forces. I felt like I was being choked by some strange fumes perhaps arising from the grenades thrown into the cells by Amin's fleeing fugitives.

The night we were freed, I heard some heavy hammering on the steel doors of Nakasero cells. I guess it was either being broken by Amin's soldiers who had lost keys and wanted to do final butchering of the detainees still alive, or they might have been the liberators (UNLA and TPDF), who were breaking the doors to set us free. I can't even tell how my friend Tumwebaze left the prison. He later told me they ran during the early hours of the morning of 11th April to their relatives in the liberated sectors of the city.

When I regained consciousness at around 2.00 pm, on 11th April, I saw several corpses in the cell where I was lying. I slowly got up with two other people, only to find the two steel doors wide open. A man who looked not to have been detained with us was cleaning the cells. He was dressed in dirty civilian clothes though. Perhaps he was a disguised Amin's agent. The man told us we were free to go! We trotted out of Nakasero with the same man. On reaching the shopping centres he joined the looters.

As we were getting out of Nakasero, some bullets were still landing in the yard, hitting at some of the vehicles belonging to Amin's soldiers who were on the run. My body and mind were still partially numbed. I was too weak to run. My underfeet were rotting because of lying in a pool of urine and faeces. Once out of the gates of Nakasero, I drank some muddy water which had collected in the potholes. It had rained heavily the previous night.

On reaching William Street flats, I was recognised by a former schoolmate at Kigezi High School, one Mwesigwa. Mwesigwa, with his sister, gave me some clean water to drink. I was given water to bathe off the mixture of clots of blood and urine.

I was also given a more decent pair of trousers to wear. Some food was served to me. Fortunately, I was able to eat a little.

Later at around 5.00pm, Mwesigwa's friends who were celebrating the liberation, offered me a lift to Makerere University, where I had been living as a non-resident student with my maternal uncle Mr Ahurwendeire, then a lecturer in the Department of Education.

It should be noted that there were two youths from Nyakishenyi, Rukungiri District, one named Karegyeya of Post Office Kabale now, and the other one a Grade II Magistrate in Ntungamo called Rubarema Frankline. They were also detained in Nakasero for one night. The two knew me. They had passed on the chilling information of my detention to my maternal uncle and the University authorities. None could at that time genuinely attempt to get me released from the fangs of death. Anyone who dared approach Nakasero would be committing unwarranted suicide.

When I was dropped at my former official hall of residence, University Hall, I proceeded to Mitchell Hall, where Mwabaze Kigya (RIP) then a student of Engineering, also hailing from Kashambya, welcomed me together with other students. I was terribly emaciated. A cousin of mine suggested they take a photo which I declined. I am told I was partially insane. I was served sodas and biscuits, which were too sweet for someone resurrecting from the dead. The taste buds were partially dead. I preferred plain water.

If I were to go into the details regarding the parental treatment given to me by Ahurwendeire, it would need a book dedicated to him. He is a professor now in Butare University, Rwanda. He cared for me, more than a father can afford to his son. He fed me well. Within a month I was bigger in size than when I was arrested.

Besides Ahurwendeire, I am grateful to the then Warden of University Hall, Mr. Gordon Kahangi, who gave me some essential foodstuffs.

Among others, I was counselled by Rev. Rutibwa (RIP) of the Department of Philosophy and Religious studies. Mr. Buyanga Beyaraaza also of Department of Philosophy, who encouraged me to keep talking about my experiences at Nakasero, so that my sagging mind could be cleared of the macabre treatment to which I was subjected for eight days.

Some students, most of them finalists, helped me a lot. They visited me often. This helped me to re-integrate into the sane, caring society. Some of them are: Mr. Rwanguha Muhwezi now of Labour Department, Jinja. Mr. Kabateraine David - Ministry of Finance & Economic Planning, Late Dr. Charles Mugoba and O.B. Kigezi H.S., Late Mbabazi Angellina then student of Social Sciences, my cousin Dr. Byabashaija Omuhunde Johnson now Assistant Commissioner and OC prisons Kigo and many others.

After recovering from the horrors of Nakasero, many of my friends advised me to apply for the so-called 'Rehabilitation Allowance' a financial scheme designed by the then UNLF returnees to rob the national treasury of the meagre foreign exchange which Amin had failed to carry as he was being fired at by the forces of freedom. I simply told my friends that no amount of material compensation could ever be a suitable substitute for man's freedom sealed in blood sacrificed by Ugandan combatants and their Tanzanian compatriots.

2
Hide and seek in the Ministry of Information

John Kihika

Major Juma Oris' courage lay in the power of the gun. Without it, he was a great coward. Some time in the mid-1970s when he was at the height of his power, as Minister of Information and Broadcasting, he wanted to address the staff of his Ministry, early in the morning. About five hundred of us assembled in the grounds of the Ministry's headquarters, on Kampala's Nakasero Hill. We were in a jovial mood, anxious to hear what our youthful Minister had to say. The jovial mood, however, changed in a twinkling of an eye.

Flanked by his Permanent Secretary and other senior officials of the Ministry, Juma Oris began to harangue the assembly at exactly 8.00am. He expressed doubt as to whether all those who worked in the Ministry supported the Military Government. He feared that some worked in the interest of former President Milton Obote who was then in exile in neighbouring Tanzania. The statement caused a stir and murmur of disapproval among the crowd. Juma Oris responded by pouring insults on the dumbfounded assembly. Disappointed that his insults bore no effects on the crowd, he pulled out a pistol and fired a bullet into the ground. He then rushed off like a mad man and disappeared in a side block of offices that had once served as a hospital. Horrified by the behaviour of their own Minister, the assembly melted in all directions, like a herd of cattle attacked by a lion. As Senior Officers in the Ministry, we had difficulty in rallying the junior members of staff to settle down at their respective places of work that day. The incident became the subject of discussion for a couple of days. By sheer luck, no one had been hurt.

By choosing to address the staff of his Ministry at 8.00 am, Juma Oris was trying to emulate Amin Dada's example. Amin used to summon Ministers and Senior Government Officials by radio to his Command Post residence at daybreak. On one such occasion, the radio announcement called upon the entire Cabinet to report with their

Permanent Secretaries the following day at 5.00 am without fail. As Director of Information, I had to make sure that the Presidential Press Unit was at Command Post well before that time to set up their gadgets in time. In conjunction with the Permanent Secretary, we arranged for the Unit to stay put in the offices for the night where they were served with food from nearby restaurants. Otherwise, how could one keep the team together to be at the command post by 4.00 am and set up their gadgets in time!

The first batch of Ministers and Permanent Secretaries arrived at about 4.45am. By then our team of reporters, photographers, television cameramen and public address system operators had their equipment well in place. The idea of keeping them in offices where they were collected in a convoy of vehicles stood us in good stead. The officials kept trickling in and by 4.55am the sizeable sitting room of the two-storey building was packed to capacity. Amin, himself, came down from upstairs at 5.00 am, as if to catch late comers. He was dressed in a blue airforce uniform with his shirt sleeves folded at the elbows. He had a matching cap on his somewhat round head. He always looked smart in his uniform.

'So you are here,' he said. 'Ha! Ha! Ha! Ha!'. With a sinister laugh in a harsh voice, he bellowed the greeting 'Good morning all of you.'

'Good morning Your Excellency,' the gathering reciprocated fearfully.

'You have come very early,' he said. 'It is very good. Anyway I have forgotten something.' He then returned upstairs and came back five minutes later with some papers in his hands.

At about the same time, an Under Secretary who stood in for his Permanent Secretary sneaked in quietly and cowered himself in a corner. But the room was too small for him to remain unnoticed. Amin's surveying eye caught up with him. Placing his papers on the table, Amin howled at him. 'You! Why don't you report?'

The now seemingly frightened man jumped to his feet.

'I have reported, Your Excellency,' he replied in a cracking voice.

'To whom?' Amin enquired again.

The man, frightened out of his wits, stammered, 'I ha-ve-ve-ve reported here sir.'

'How have you reported?' Amin asked him.

The man stood puzzled with his mouth open like a constipated bull, his eyes rolling uncontrollably in their sockets, like wheels of a grinding mill. While some naughty members of the Press Unit almost cracked their ribs with controlled laughter, a sympathetic TV cameraman who stood near him tugged at his trembling trousers and advised him, 'Greet him.'

The man gathered courage and greeted the President with a shout, 'Good morning, Your Excellency,'

'Yes,' Amin replied with satisfaction adding, 'You must report when you come in.' Of course, parallel lines never meet. While Amin spoke military language, the man spoke ordinary English.

Meanwhile, a long serving Permanent Secretary entered the room. His mouth was half-open and he was sweating profusely. He looked like a man coming out of a swimming pool. Amin spotted him and accosted him.

'Why are you late?' he asked, diverting his attention from the Under Secretary.

The new arrival replied in a hoarse voice, 'My car had a puncture.'

'What punture? the President enquired omitting the letter "c" in the word puncture.

The now nervous man adjusted his jacket and said, 'I mean the tyre of my car went flat, just near Kololo Airstrip and I had to walk here,'

Amin seemed convinced by the school-like lie.

Late comers out of the way, Amin went straight to business. He addressed his audience heartily, thanking his listeners for the good job they were doing. He then came to the point why he had summoned them to Command Post.

'I think you Ministers, you are on leave, isn't it a true?' he asked rhetorically, as if he had discussed the matter with them before. A spell of silence clamped on the audience like a steel door.

'Yes,' Amin went on, 'You are tired and the whole Ministers must rest. Each Ministers you must carry out proper hand over to your Permanent Secretaries immediately and you must go on leave for one month. Permanent Secretary, you are all of you now acting Minister, isn't it true?' he asked rhetorically again. By now the sun was out and he invited us all to breakfast. Waiters from Nile Hotel were by then waiting outside to carry out their assignment.

The idea of the Presidential Press Unit or P.P.U. as it was popularly known, was mooted way back in 1972 by the Permanent Secretary, Ministry of Information and Broadcasting. A very able administrator, he realised Amin's daily engagements and those of his wives which he always wanted publicised, called for a special press team. The Permanent Secretary, in consultation with this Minister, set aside three of the best of each: news reporters, photographers, television cameramen plus public address system operators to form the P.P.U. which he put under my charge, with two vehicles and their drivers at my disposal. By then I had not yet been promoted to Director of Information. They created a post of Chief Information Officer to which I was promoted. The Permanent Secretary took the earliest opportunity to introduce my Unit to President Amin at Command Post, and he liked the idea.

Within a matter of days, we were required to travel to Arua town in West Nile where Amin had arranged to address a public rally. I decided to attend and report the rally myself so as to set an example to my juniors. Before it began, Amin instructed me to write everything he would say. About five hundred people attended the rally, half of them soldiers in their uniforms. It began at 10.00 am. Amin spoke in his halting English while three people interpreted his speech into three local languages namely Alur, Lugbara and Kakwa. At first his speech was all right and it seemed sensible for me to make a verbatim report. Towards the middle, however, Amin become erratic. At one point he said, 'The whole people must understand that I do everything good for the whole soldiers.' He would mention an individual soldier's name and take pains to enumerate everything he had done for him during that soldier's military career.

'So and so,' he would say, 'I promoted him to sergeant; I sent him to such Military Academy. I promoted him to sergeant major' and so on. He would then mention another soldier's name and go through the same process. Some twenty to thirty names were mentioned. It was then that I realised that there had been a military uprising in the offing among military personnel from West Nile which Amin was trying to quell.

In my naivety, I thought my job was to be a service to the people through the mass media - radio, television and the press generally for whom I was reporting not to Amin as such. I therefore left out of his speech all that I considered trash and I put down only all that was consumable by the people as a whole. In spite of that, by the time the rally ended, just after 4.00pm, I had filled a complete shorthand notebook writing on both sides of each leaf.

Immediately after the rally, he ordered me to meet him in his hotel room at Rhino Hotel, where he asked me to transcribe and read to him in English the report I was going to transmit to the Ministry Headquarters. Not only was the report not ready, it lacked the details he wanted. He became furious and assigned a certain Brigadier Musa Hussein who had flanked him at the rally to help me transcribe and write a report for him to read. Naturally, this was a mission impossible for the soldier who did not hesitate to report back to Amin his failure to accomplish the task. At the height of his fury, Amin ordered me to abandon my team I had travelled with to Arua by road and secured me a seat on his six seater plane in order to fly back to Kampala with him the following day. On the plane, he used all vulgar words one could think of to insult me, saying I was a dangerous man who worked for Obote. He threatened to kill and make me disappear. I had once hunted and killed a wounded buffalo before and that was preferable to meeting Amin at the height of his fury.

Once in Kampala, he summoned the Minister of Information and the Permanent Secretary to his office in Parliament Building where he told them what I had done. He grabbed the summarised report I had prepared about the rally and ordered me to get out of his office. While I staggered home on foot, he used the report to recollect what he said at the rally and dictated the whole speech to his personal secretaries. At that time news bulletins were limited to fifteen minutes on radio and television. That evening the bulletin comprised only of one item: Amin's rally in Arua. It lasted more than an hour on both radio and television.

On their return to the Ministry, both the Minister and the P.S. jointly gave me stern instructions never to appear before Amin again.

'The man is very serious,' they emphasised. 'If you try to appear before him, your will be in trouble.' However knowing that I was the most suitable person for the job in the Ministry, they declined to relieve me of the responsibility of heading the Presidential Press Unit. They assured me I made the report the way it should have been, adding, 'But you know the sort of person Amin is.'

They advised me to administer the P.P.U from behind the scenes and to send him other people whenever he wanted a coverage team, but never to appear before him myself. I hid all this carefully from my wife who I knew would have urged me to go to exile, the thing I never wanted to do.

I obeyed my superior's instructions for about three months. Then came a time when I could not obey them anymore. Amin and his wives had many engagements one day and the P.P.U was overstretched. I managed to raise a photographer and cameraman for one of the functions, but I totally failed to raise a reporter. They were all too busy preparing their reports. Without telling the Minister or the Permanent Secretary, I took the risk and went as a reporter myself.

What a surprise! Amin was overjoyed at seeing me. He had shot and killed a hippopotamus the previous night, on the shores of Lake Victoria. The next day he summoned Ministers, Permanent Secretaries and other senior government officials at the site perhaps to demonstrate his prowess. On seeing me among the gathering, he embarrassed me by exclaiming

'Kihika, where have been all this time? It's a long time.'

By chance, I managed to think of a lie, 'I have been on a long leave, Your Excellency,'

'Now it is over?' he enquired.

'Yes, it is over, Your Excellency.'

'Yes, he said automatically. 'That is good.'

There was nothing like a function, other than Amin pointing to the spot where he claimed to have shot the best with a single bullet. The carcass was no longer at the scene. He claimed he had given it to the villagers for meat. The simple ceremony ended with a reception in style at the Cape Town Villas thereafter.

I had no difficulty in appearing at other functions where Amin officiated, making sure to avoid any other ugly confrontations with him. I also realised, however, that in spite of his ferocious behaviour, Amin could forgive and forget. He is a human being after all.

Many of the Ministers who Amin sent on leave without notice did not return to their posts. After a period of one month, some were transferred to other ministries while others were dropped altogether. The Minister who had played a protective role in my favour was among the casualties who lost their jobs. In his place Amin put Captain Juma Oris whom he later promoted to major while still Minister of Information. He had just returned from military training in Pakistan.

One afternoon, Juma Oris and I returned from lunch at the same time. He was driving himself in a personal car. I parked mine a short distance from his and as I was making the car secure, he yelled a greeting to me. I returned the greeting respectfully, drawing nearer to him.

'How are things?' he asked.

'Fine sir,' I replied.

'How many wives do you have?'

'Only one, sir,' I said.

'When will you marry another one?' he enquired further.

'I don't intend to,' I responded.

'Why not, is one wife enough?'

When I confirmed in the affirmative, Juma Oris came to the point and said: 'Anyway, when will you, Kihika, become a Muslim?'

I lost control of myself and said, 'What? Me becoming a Muslim?'

He asked 'Why not?'

Pointing to a tree near where I had parked my car, I said emphatically, 'Before anyone turns me into a Muslim, one will first have to nail me on that tree.'

When Juma Oris asked why, I replied, 'That is one of the things I don't believe in.'

This made him very furious and he started insulting me. 'How can you speak that, you stupid man. You speak like that again, I'll beat you.'

I returned his threat, 'If you beat me, I will beat you too. I'm not a woman.'

At that, he hurried off the scene like a child stung by a bee and disappeared into the nearby office building. I thought he would return with a gun and shoot me. He did not.

Amin used the radio and T.V time allocated for comment sometimes to attack and insult other heads of state, the Queen of England and Mwalimu Julius Nyerere of Tanzania included. State House Entebbe would ring to tell us that there would be a comment coming to be used that day. Later a driver would arrive to deliver a well written and punctuated comment in fluent English. We always wondered who wrote those comments.

An occasion arose, however, when Amin had to be on the receiving end. As he was busy hosting the OAU Heads of State and Government Summit in Kampala in July 1975, news came that President Yakubu Gowon of Nigeria had been overthrown in a military coup. Gowon abandoned the summit immediately and headed for London. I took opportunity of the fact that all eyes and ears in Amin's State Research were focused on the summit and I wrote a daring comment attacking Amin without mentioning his name directly. I wrote that the overthrow of Gowon was a lesson to those African leaders who thought that leadership in their respective countries was the presence of one man. I reminded them of the saying that where grass is burned, fresh grass grows and it is always better than old grass. I went on to explain that no country ever runs short of a leader. That no sooner a leader goes, another comes on to the scene.

Considering that Amin had declared himself 'Life President', one could imagine the kind of risk I ran by writing and having such scathing attack broadcast on government radio and television, when a record number of African leaders were assembled in Kampala. I don't know how it escaped the notice of Amin's security cronies. I think I was right in thinking that all their eyes and ears were focused on the summit, otherwise I would not have been alive today. The following weekend, I heard people discussing the comment at a party. They were all hopeful that Amin was about to be overthrown.

'Did you hear the comment on radio, and how much it attacked African dictators?' one of the men asked enthusiastically. 'I'm sure a very powerful man must have authorised it up in high echelon of the military! Otherwise who could have allowed something like that to be broadcast on government radio!'

I quietly pitied the man for entertaining false hopes. I wish he knew how powerless to the extent of being useless the author of the comment was. Eventually when we had to publish a collection of those comments in a book form, I made sure the offensive paragraph was removed; so that it did not remain on permanent record.

On another occasion, I used the same comment to attack banks, which were very inefficient at that time, especially Uganda Commercial Bank, where one could hardly spend less than two hours to transact simple banking business. I suggested in the comment that banks should extend their business hours well into the afternoon if the morning period was not sufficient for them. This must have been taken as a presidential directive in the banking circles and within a few weeks banks began to operate on Saturdays up to midday; while on other days business extended up to 3.00pm. However, as soon as Amin was overthrown, they reverted to their old arrangement of operating up to 12.30pm. While the Saturday arrangement was scrapped altogether.

Putting this in perspective one might see how much damage might have been done in the name of Amin while he was not aware during his regime. I am not saying he did not do awful things himself. I think, however, most crimes were committed in his name by people who took advantage of his inability to control the situation to settle old scores.

Sometime in 1977 the Permanent Secretary who had shielded me in conjunction with the Minister against Amin's sinister motives, decided to go on leave against my advice because I had learnt through contacts that Amin sought to replace people like him with persons of his own faith. On his departure, a radio news-reader was appointed to succeed the out-going Permanent Secretary. Before he took office, the newcomer had to be introduced by Juma Oris to a cross section of Ministry staff. The Board Room was packed for the occasion and Oris made one of his silly remarks in his introductory speech. He said, among others, that those who had served in the Ministry for a long time, people like Kihika, who thought they were indispensable, should learn by that occasion that it is time that they went. They could also be displaced.

At the end of his speech, we put out our hands, and Oris picked up a person at will to pledge loyalty and support to the new Permanent Secretary. Among the directors in the Ministry, I was the most senior. After giving a chance to the other two directors, he went on to select junior officers, some under my department, to pledge their support. He ignored my hand, although I sat hardly four feet away from him. By the time he called upon me to speak, I was visibly enraged and I could not hide my anger. I concluded my pledge and loyalty to the Permanent Secretary by telling Oris in his face that his remark that people like myself will also have to leave the Ministry was not called for. I told him that the chair I occupied – by that time I was audibly tapping on it – was not my father's chair. I had not bequeathed it from my father and the time would come when I would have to vacate it. In fact, I went on to say, I was preparing to vacate it.

At that time Oris was in Amin's best books. He had been appointed substantive Minister of Land and Water Resources after the murder of Minister Oryema. At the same time, he was holding the portfolio of the Minister of Foreign Affairs, after the disgrace of Elizabeth Bagaya of Toro and that of Information and Broadcasting, which he had vacated previously. Rumour was also rife that Amin was about to create a new post of Prime Minister to which Oris would be appointed.

So I reminded Juma Oris that according to the laws of physics, any heavy object thrown up into the air had of necessity to come down with a bang. The higher one threw it, the heavier the bang. He got the message and sprang from the chair, as if he had been given an electric shock. He poured insults on me, which I was used to anyway, saying I was a mad man. How could I, otherwise a senior officer speak like that. He picked up his baton, for he always wore military uniform and stampeded out of the boardroom like a tank moving into action. The whole assembly followed him and the meeting ended in disarray. Senior officials who still remembered the shooting incident at the assembly, blamed me for behaving in a manner that could have caused them a problem.

The portfolio of the Minister of Information and Broadcasting remained substantively vacant. After the Permanent Secretary had settled down in his new job, he decided to stage a coup. An occasion arose when, receiving a diplomat who paid a courtesy call on him, the Permanent Secretary instructed a reporter who covered the meeting for the mass media to refer to him as the acting minister. On hearing the news, Oris stopped coming to the ministry. Weeks later, we met at one of Amin's receptions at Nile Mansions Gardens. Oris asked me, surrounded by my junior members of staff, who appointed the Permanent Secretary 'acting Minister'. We made fun of him, saying the man had staged a successful coup while the one supposed to challenge him had played the coward. Juma Oris was not amused. By then it was too late for him to mount a challenge. That began Juma Oris' descent from the pinnacle of power which was completed by the joint invasion of Uganda by liberators from Tanzania, who overthrew Amin's regime in April 1979.

Soon after Amin had been ousted, the new Minister of Information asked me to act as Permanent Secretary, following the detention of the substantive Permanent Secretary who had been Amin's appointee. I had hardly served for a month in the post when Prof. Yusuf Lule who had succeeded Amin was himself overthrown by the National Consultative Council which served as parliament at that time.

In the confusion that followed, I found myself without a news editor. I decided to edit the news bulletin for the day personally. Hardly had I handled a news report than a company of soldiers stormed the news room. They were being led by a member of television staff who pointed at me saying, 'that is the man.' The soldiers led me at gun point from the news room to a convoy of waiting vehicles in the car park. I was ordered to sit in a Landrover which was packed with soldiers who pointed their guns at me. This was led by a pick-up while another followed at the back, both filled with armed soldiers.

The overthrow of Amin had been followed by a spate of killings of senior Government officials. So, when I was dragged out of the news room I thought my own end had come at last. As the vehicles that took me wound their way along the Nakasero Hill roads, I was sure that my dear wife and children would never see me again. Eventually we ended up in Nile Hotel where another group of soldiers waited in a room upstairs. Then my captors introduced me as the Permanent Secretary, Ministry of Information who had been confusing the nation on radio and television. One of the soldiers, possibly their leader whom we found waiting, ordered that I be taken to Nakasero. I was hustled back to the Landrover that waited in the car park still packed with armed soldiers. From there I was driven to a residential house west of All Saints Church. But inside, it served as a prison. Two soldiers led me past scores of detainees, lying on the floor, many of them half naked. I knew if I was spared from death that day, the best I could expect was to join the miserable group. The thought scared me stiff. In an inner room sat a soldier behind a desk. He was cordial, polite and more understanding than any of the soldiers I had encountered in my ordeal so far. I was made to understand that his name was Captain Anthony.

My captors repeated the accusations. As one of them ripped my watch off my wrist, the captain ordered him to return it to me. I pocketed it for safety. The captain asked me to explain to him how and why I had been arrested and where they had found me. I told him the latter but could not explain my arrest. He did not seem to believe the accusations. So he picked up a phone and sought advice from the Chief of Staff as to how to deal with me.

Apparently the Chief of Staff had instructed Captain Anthony to obtain a written statement from me detailing the cause and manner of my arrest. After which I should be allowed to go home, returning the next day when a decision would be made on whether to detain me or set me free. After carefully writing the statement, the captain asked me to go home. He offered a vehicle which I declined, afraid the driver was one of those detailed to destroy me. As I walked home, I wondered how I would face my wife. It was approaching 7.00pm when I left detention. My arrest had been effected at around 3.00pm. On arrival at home, I found a sympathiser conferring with my wife where to look for me. He had heard of my arrest and he broke the news to her. They were relieved to see me. On my part, I had difficulty in stifling back tears of – what I don't know – from my eyes. All along I had been pitying my wife, knowing she was unaware of what I was going through.

The following day, I clothed myself heavily in preparation for detention. When I reported to the captain, however, he surprised me by telling me to go and resume my work normally. He said the Chief of Staff had found nothing in my report or anywhere else warranting my arrest. Nevertheless, he warned me that there might be rivalry at the place of work either due to women or connected with my position of employment. As time went on, it transpired that people were after my job.

These engineered all sorts of machinations not only to push me out of the Ministry, but the civil service as well. One of them was that, as a Permanent Secretary, I had issued a press card to a journalist whose planned magazine later came out with an article that was critical to President Binaisa's Government. I came to learn that the matter went even up to the Cabinet where like during the days of Amin, I was described as a saboteur who should be pushed out of the Ministry, investigated and detained if necessary. A sympathetic cabinet minister, formerly a civil servant, who participated in the deliberations was appalled to see me on Kampala Road. He asked me what I was doing in Kampala. Otherwise I would be arrested. Once again I hid this again from my wife, fearing she would urge me to go into exile. Instead, I went to the countryside after convincing her that finishing touches had to be put to our country home which was under construction.

When Binaisa's Government was eventually overthrown, I made attempts to return to my job, not as acting Permanent Secretary but as Director of Information. I still met resistance from both the Minister and Permanent Secretary. So I continued on forced leave with full pay, until my conscience bothered me for continuing to draw salary for which I was not working. I went back after spending a period of two years in the wilderness to have my position clarified. By then, the country was half way into the Obote II regime.

When I asked why a small fly like me was being harassed so much, the Permanent Secretary did not mince his words. He told me plainly: 'We want your post,' he said. Explaining further, 'You see, by religion, you are not one of us. By politics you are out of our grouping. Therefore, we want you out so that we can fill your post with our own person.' He instructed me to fill in a retirement form which I was to hand to him within a month. Failing to do so, they would resort to other means to ensure that the post was made vacant. I refused to meet the deadline. He then sent me a letter urging me to comply.

While I became bitter with the man for the unusual manner he handled my case, I was nevertheless grateful to him for enabling me to quit the civil service alive. Otherwise, I would have been eliminated like other senior civil servants who had been murdered in cold blood. Anyway, my theory was once again at work: a heavy object had been thrown up into air and it had come down with a bang. It all began the day I was made acting Permanent Secretary.

Thus ended my civil career that spanned a period of nearly thirty years, full of happy but also nasty experiences. It was, nevertheless, not all that easy.

3
The murder of Nekemia Bananuka
Elia Georges Muhindi

His penis had been chopped off and planted in his mouth. 'He smokes his pipe,' they mocked. His testicles had been slashed and deposited on a plate and given him named 'chips and sausages.' His blood had been trapped in a cup and forced into his mouth, saying it was holy wine.

Who was doing all that? It was the soldiers of Idi Amin and the year was 1972. To who? To Nekemia Bananuka, former general secretary of Ankole, in the Obote I Administration.

Bananuka was my foster father and a husband of my aunt Robinah Keitumba, sister to my father, Muhindi Dominic. He had been a UPC activist prior to his death, and a man of zeal and energy, with a heart of unequalled kindness, especially when it came to children.

He was arrested at around 3.00pm. on a Saturday in 1972, from a granary of his sister Ruth, where he was hiding. I was ten years old then.

The sister's home which was in Rugando-Rwampara, some 12 miles from his home of Ruharo in Mbarara was a converient hiding place for him from Amin's thugs, on rampage after the 1972 Tanzanian invasion of Mbarara.

On his way to the other end of the world, Bananuka was bound in a heap, webbed up in ropes and wrapped into a ball. When he said he was extra-ordinarily tall for the boot to swallow him, his tormentors proposed another solution to their project - the solution was a hammer which they used to pound his limbs, arms and joints to get a shape out of him reasonable enough to gather in a sack and load in a car boot for Idi Amin to certify that Bananuka was truly dead.

But death alone wasn't enough – Bananuka's head was wanted as a souvenir in Amin's freezer, to remind him that enemies of his Government were getting less at every count of a new head. Yes, it was chopped off and preserved thus.

Bananuka's death was followed by the deaths of his three sons (my beloved cousins) who were arrested while trying to escape to our aunt

Violet Buriiro, then a primary teacher at Kazo Primary School, some 20 miles from Ibanda town.

In Ibanda town, also, was one of our cousins, Christian Kyikonyogo who was working as a nurse at Ibanda Health Center. The three cousins had planned to hide at one of the two places for immediate safety and then plan their journey to Dar-es-Salaam.

But the plans for exile never materialised. The three were arrested before arrival in Ibanda town, assembled in one line and showered with torrents of bullets.

Killed were Cadet Bananuka who had just completed 'O' level at Kituunga High School and joined Ntare School for the 'A' level; David Bananuka who had graduated at Makerere University Kampala with a Bachelor of Commerce (Hon); and Herbert Bananuka Munarura, who was working with Uganda Commercial Bank, Mbarara Branch. They were the three I had shared childhood pleasures and joys with. I had been adopted by the Bananuka family after my parents separated in 1962.

During the abortive guerrilla invasion of 1972, I had by coincidence been sent to my mother Angela Kembabi for a visit. She lived in Rugando, Rwampara where she had obtained herself some land and built a house. Even here, Bananuka's name haunted us. He was a man most wanted by Idi Amin.

But Bananuka was no coward. Sometimes he took risks that displeased members of his family. When Tanzanians sporadically shot at Mbarara, the family escaped in disarray, but due to his love for children, he risked not going far, and shortly stole himself back home to check on the whereabouts of his children.

He escaped death narrowly from advancing Amin's soldiers, driving to his home for him. As a risk taker, Bananuka managed to hide in a drum before he was noticed by the advancing enemies. The soldiers took no effort to search for him, they seemed pretty sure he had fled! They had their revenge by looting all his property, and showering bullets at his house in massive destruction of window panes.

After they were gone Bananuka fled his drum. His destination was his sister Ruth's house in Rugando, Rwampara, who hid him in her granary. The granary was also near my mother's home and we bid a farewell to our beloved with a meal we smuggled to him for only one night.

That night, Bananuka planned to escape to Tanzania to exile. The plans aborted because the son of his sister Ruth by name of Rupiiha tipped off Amin's soldiers in Mbarara of Bananuka's whereabouts and they immediately picked him. Rupiiha had hoped to inherit his uncle's wealth after his death and for that reason had given the enemy the desired information. So there ended Bananuka, never to be seen again.

After this, Mbarara became a blood thirsty desert. Executions at Kakyeka stadium became the order of the day. Fear and panic swept the region. A terrifying personality cult ensued with Idi Amin proclaiming himself President for life.

And of course silence under tides of new laws in the form of decrees and proclamations! Some of these laws empowered the public to castrate thieves and suspects and squeeze life out of their bodies. Mysterious disappearances became common.

As the country became a pool of blood, another death took another relation of the Bananuka family. This was my aunt Katalina, sister of my mother who took care of Bananuka's property after his death. She had been warned of a planned arrest by the soldiers and hid herself at a friend's home in Katojo, Ruti trading centre, Mbarara. Here she was followed by military men, butchered along with her friend, wrapped in blankets and locked in the house to rot and decompose.

It was not until the bodies were fully decomposed that the village risk-takers broke into the house and pulled out their rot for burial in a single grave. The pollution that choked the air then can't be described in any words.

The danger of wiping out the entire Bananukas was so great that we saw no alternative but to scatter up. My aunt Robinah Bananuka contemplated fleeing to exile in Dar-es-Salaam. But we had to get rid of the gun hidden in the ceiling of our house. The task of retrieving the gun from the hiding place fell to me as I was the smallest. In fact I seized it carelessly unable to think it could explode in my face if touched at the wrong place. And when I deposited it to the floor, my aunt stared at it in terror, possibly thinking it could explode.

We buried the gun in the swamp overlooking our stock-farm, and covered it with soil, stones and mud. After this duty, my aunt breathed a sigh of relief.

How my aunt reached Dar-es-Salaam is a story that will die with herself. All we know is that she left us planning to cross Kagera to Tanzania via Kikagate where a ferry stands. The only time we came to hear of her again was at the advent of the UNLF administration when exiles returned en masse to their country a decade since Idi Amin. And when she returned, she was not only a changed woman but also a doomed one. Her days of suffering and memories of lost children and husband had totally damaged her mind and turned her to a recluse who couldn't easily be reached and talked to.

Meanwhile after my aunt had left for Tanzania other escapes followed. They were of her son George Bananuka who was at Kings College Budo in a final advanced class and Darlison Kyokutamba, her daughter, who was studying at Kyambogo Teachers College.

George Bananuka, penniless that time, walked all his way to Dar-es-Salaam, via Mutukula - a journey that took him more than a month. George's survival stood at the mercy of strangers - especially in Tanzania - where he had little fear to seek their sympathies. Some of the time, he obtained lifts from sympathisers as he walked his way on dusty roads to Dar-es-Salaam, where he joined his brother Fred Bananuka, who was doing his Bachelor of Commerce at the University. From Dar-es-Salaam, George was well placed with the Obote group exiles, and this connection obtained him a scholarship to London University, where he later became a barrister at law.

Now the only child left of the Bananuka's direct blood was Darlison Kyokutamba who was at hanging point of getting butchered had she not been witty enough to fall under friends of Amin's camp. Darlison, naturally an enterprising genius, took for herself a man who was a Muslim and fellow student, in a marriage that gave them five children. Darlison's enterprising behaviour, characteristic of her father, prompted her to finance her Muslim man into a profitable shoes import business called May Fair - then at Jinja Road - which flourished beyond imaginable proportions. The business collapsed after a decade and a half in 1985 when her marriage broke up. As to why there came a divorce will remain a secret between Darlison and her man, Solomon.

Anyhow after these exiles and counter exiles, the rest of us, orphans, found ourselves lost, helpless, hopeless and homeless. Under these conditions, I was re-adopted by a relative, social worker Francis Katsigazi at Kinoni Saza headquarters.

Katsigazi had social responsibilities he offered at Kinoni but I for sure can't tell what they entailed. What I remember is that he was involved in educating homeless children in how to read, write and count.

And what I remember for sure again the classroom had no other learners, except me. And I don't remember there were any books or pencils. Our writing, which was purely by finger, was done in heaps of dust, spread on levelled surfaces. The other lessons included counting stones, then graduation.

After my graduation from dust, some sympathisers observed that I had a great potential for language and counting and there undertook to meet some of my school fees, until they saw me through high school and college.

But there was none left before us to share joys of early days. Bananuka – my beloved foster father – was dead. My beloved cousins were dead. My aunt - sister to my mother - was dead. The few of us were scattered in disarray like the stampede of charging wolves. The shadows of darkness had thus dwelt before us and their ends hung unknown.

4
To Russia Without Love

Tumusiime Encebebe

'Spassiba bolishoi!' This was a phrase I mastered in the Russian language long before I boarded a plane to Moscow in 1975. It had been arranged clandestinely to disguise myself simply by talking a foreign language at the airport. To speak the English language, one would be overheard and consequently get cross-examined; to indulge in any of the local dialects would betray one's tribe and the henchmen were quite prepared to stick a spy on you. I knew some bit of French but this was hopeless; Amin's men and women in State Research came from Tripoli, Kigali and Kinshasa - I would betray my ethnicity. The soldiers in civilian uniform were posted everywhere to grab guerrillas from Tanzania. Fair-skinned Banyankore, Bakiga, Banyoro and Batoro were directly linked to the invaders at Mutukula in 1972. So it was not safe to reveal your tribe when leaving the country lest you were deemed Dar-es-Salaam bound. Anyone leaving the country had to be cleared by security organs. In this particular period any traveller whose name resembled mine was not safe. The henchmen had short-listed me for questioning at either Nakasero or Makindye or both places or none of these. The shores of Lake Victoria or the Nile River or even Namanve thickets would have served quite nicely.

I had to leave the country or face the music. So with a few close friends who made thorough homework for my escape, we decided that I leave Uganda via Entebbe Airport. The exercise was rigorous and demanded patience, and stamina was exactly what we all needed. To pass through the airport, you had to keep talking steadily in a language to be understood by the 'officials' at the airport but puzzling to the soldiers in civilian uniform.

Now what was this civilian uniform? The State Research boys used to dress uniquely. It was a simple attire equivalent to today's safari suit but with long sleeves. Inside the Kaunda suit was concealed a pistol of some calibre and either a nylon rope or handcuffs or even a sharp blade. Most of the squadron leaders were of the Nubian descent whose cheeks had several slashes engraved on them by primitive razor operations, resembling upright strokes, three or four abreast. We therefore nicknamed them 'one, one, one' or 'one hundred eleven' or just 'a thousand strokes'! These were the murder squads who abducted and killed people at leisure, the people who delighted in compacting *wanainchi* in tiny car-boots on their way to the slaughter houses all over the country. These people were dreaded everywhere by everyone. They themselves would be assigned duties to clobber fellow henchmen who messed: to miss a targeted victim meant your own throat being twisted! Their 'uniform' was of all shades and so indeed simpletons would wear similar designs innocently. These chaps went everywhere - bars, hotels, schools, shops, farms and buses. They included houseboys, drivers, teachers, professors, diplomats. All in all, these were the people in front of whose faces I marched into exile.

The state research boys had a duty to cover Ingrid Hills' house day and night to see who came and went. She stayed in the flats off Livingstone Terrace at Makerere University near the present Faculty of Technology, on the second floor. This woman was the wife of Denis Hills who had written *The White Pumpkin* and was arrested by Amin. The chaos which followed was widely covered in the press. While a student at Makerere University Kampala, I was privileged to coach her seven year old son together with Rachel and Michael - the kids of late Michael Kawalya Kaggwa who had been found burnt in his Mercedes sports car at Nakulabye. His wife was a European and she lived near Athina Club Kololo. On different days I would coach the three in her house.

On more than three occasions these guys would ask me which flat I had come from. Probably my arrogance saved me because I was a confident fellow with B.Sc. Dip. Ed. Certificate by choice and not allocation. Moreover there was no way I could suspect any danger because at my hall of residence (Livingstone) I employed a chap or two to do odd jobs for me like weekend laundry and room polishing or newspaper collection from Wandegeya to be slipped under the door. Indeed I mistook these young men for job-seekers - but then State Research boys were capable of any chores as long as they got someone's neck cracked. Denis Hills was staying near Summit view at Kololo.

One night I was stone-broke and I wanted some quid very badly. I rang Mrs. Hills at around 8.00pm and she told me to run on up and collect my allowance as she was on her way to dine some place. The telephone booth was near the custodian's window and my room A15 was upstairs, also near the reception at the entrance. Now I practically bolted and literally ran uphill to the flats, I did notice three faces on my errand for payment. They were not foreign to me but again not familiar. It was darkish but surely these were the chaps I had met some days earlier on my way from coaching. The time being night, this made me jittery.

So I went to Mrs. Hills' flat and found her ready to move out. She went to a drawer (I was not asked to sit down), pulled out the money in her palm, went to the window overlooking the drive-in and drew the curtains slowly and carefully. After a while, she let the curtain go, sighed heavily, came to me and handed me the money. She then asked me if I wanted a lift to Wandegeya as she was going that way. I obliged. I noticed she was perturbed all the way to the shopping arcade. She did not talk much and her eyes hovered in the tree shades suspiciously. Was she looking for anyone?

Mrs. Ingrid Hills dropped me near the Wandegeya round about and told me to take care of myself - to me that was European jargon. I went to the College Inn and bought a packet of Embassy cigarettes. It is at this time that I noticed I did not have the keys to my room because I had a diamond lighter affixed to the bunch. I was not going to booze without my keys and so homeward I had to return.

When I reached the custodian's place, I saw the same young chaps talking to him. I went up to my room to find my keys without the fancy lighter. Certainly someone had removed it from the key-holder, this was obvious. I rushed to the Custodian's place downstairs and finding him not busy (the other two chaps had vanished), I enquired whether he had seen my roommate or anyone ask for me. 'What did the two boys want?' 'They were three but one of them had gone to Block D when you passed here. They seem to have gone off in a hurry when you went upstairs. What is more, they asked for your name - they said they are book sellers'.

I went back to my room and made sure it was locked. I made my way to the University Canteen wondering what the hell these blokes wanted to sell to me. From the canteen I found a few friends and we decided to hire a taxi to Susanna Night Club in Nakulabye. This was a Friday but then I had practical physics sessions every Saturday from 8.00am. to 12.00 noon. I danced a few hits and decided to desert my colleagues without notice. I had initiated the voyage and was at a loss to give in so early.

When I reached Livingstone hall, the custodian was alert enough to stop me and tense-say, 'I say, one of the boys came here twice in the company of some other fellows who do not belong to the hall. I am sure I saw them checking the list over there and it is possible they went upstairs. Maybe he concluded, 'they were looking for you.'

'What did they say?'

'Nothing to me.'

'How did they look like?'

'Like you; not drunk.'

So I was sober. I became uneasy. That Kaunda suit entourage for me - the Mobutu attire which concealed weapons underneath! I panicked. To conceal my confusion I told the custodian that I was going back to look for cigarettes at the C.C.B - Centres for Continuing Booze. This was the place to which we heavy weights retired after the closure of the canteen at 10.00pm. In those days, you either went for the bottle under the bed - the equivalent of today's 24-hour open Kafundas – or you went to a night club. Though popular now, these joints were notorious in the 70's. Even so, fear gripped me and I found myself walking to Bombo Road flats near Odeon Cinema where my sister Ziwa was lodging with her husband Simeo.

Nyansio, one of the friends I had left at the Susanna Night Club was approached by a young man who informed him I was in trouble outside the dancing hall and that I needed assistance. Nyansio rushed outside to relieve me. This was in the middle of a rumba jazz, so he did not alert Jim - the other campuser from New Hall. Once outside, Nyansio was forcibly persuaded into a waiting vehicle where he found a girl sitting in the front seat. He later narrated how they pounced on him demanding my whereabouts. He believes he took them to many places that night where he thought I could have gone. He is still alive but does not recall much. He was found by garbage collectors the following afternoon on Lugogo By-pass. I gather he stopped talking to anyone for many months! He was to graduate with the name 'Mandevu the silent.'

When I reached my sister's house at around two o'clock in the middle of the night, she refused to open to me. I was a hard drinker and so was her hubby Simeo. She must have thought it was one of our drinking sprees in the offing. My dear friend was not at home, she said. If I could walk from Susanna Night Club to Livingstone Hall (I had not told her I had walked that stretch), and that if I got scared stiff enough to walk to the city centre (Odeon is not in the city centre), I was at liberty to walk back to Makerere or indeed walk straight on to Jajja Marina, the way I sounded frightened. There was no breakfast for me even if I cared to hang around till daylight so - please go! Jesus come!

I was thinking about nothing just then when I heard car tyres screech somewhere on the road. On impulse I fled by the hind entrance into a gulley and made for Bakuli direction. I sprinted past Gardenia Hotel, down into the valley and up Namirembe Road for my life! When I reached the market, I hid behind a small bar in the urinal. I used to frequent that joint so I knew the corners well. I am not sure I should mention here that I saw a speeding car zoom by and I cannot write with authority that I saw a UVS number plate through a slit in the toilet. The vehicle for Mengo Hospital or whatever other destination.

As I listened to my bejewelled Timex Watch (ticker-timer Timex), I marked time. Soon the dials glittered to show 4.30am and now the people of Owino Market started to wheel steaming food downwards from obscure corners.

I had now calmed down enough to join the throng of market vendors and thus walked back to the bus park.

Meanwhile I was later to learn that some people visited my sister's flat and not finding any man inside, she was beaten to a pulp and left for dead - thanks to her screaming kids, Roger and Gordon.

I boarded the first town service bus to Bweyogerere and alighted at Banda. My friend Ben was a teacher at Kyambogo College School, House No. 6, also a flat upstairs. I asked for money and he gave me 500/- suspiciously. In addition he volunteered to ride to Makerere and collect my briefcase which contained my passport and a few other certificates. He later came back without a briefcase - he thought it wise to leave it in place, just in case. As far as my roommate was concerned, there was nothing amiss when he came from his weekend in Mbale. The roommate of mine was a born-again Christian and took it for granted that I had run crazy with booze in some place - a phenomenon not quite uncommon.

With the 500/= and the passport, I left Ben and disappeared in thin air as we drank potent gin in the suburbs of Kyambogo. I then started walking along the railway line from the present Pepsi Cola plant, through Nakawa, the railway station, Nalukolongo, to Kyengera on Masaka road. I joined Mityana road somewhere after Busega roundabout near Temangalo and hailed a Mubende bound taxi.

It is true my brother worked in Mityana as a District Forest Officer but his home was not my destination. I did however need his contact later and subsequent financial aid but not now. What I needed now was to disappear. Let it be known by State Research boys that their target had vanished. One group or individual was to claim responsibility for my eradication in return for higher favours.

My friend Akiiki, an old schoolmate, welcomed and 'sealed' me in his garage. He responded very quickly to the cause. Earlier on in the year, I had attended and passed an interview for a scholarship to study in the Soviet Union. We used to underrate Russian Degrees in our 'academic circle'. So I was not eager to leave campus and go to Siberia. There was still time to present our passport at the Soviet Embassy before July for visas. This Mutoro man who had been to Eastern Europe several times said we Africans looked the same on photographs. He borrowed a camera and photographed me. He then removed the film and returned the camera to the owner. He grabbed my passport and went to Kampala. In the garage, he left me roasted cassava, a packet of biscuits, a tin of clean water, a basin and Vim. So the cabin was self contained - toilet was substituted for by the basin.

Three days later he returned. He had the visa. He had been inoculated for cholera and yellow fever and presented me the required certificates for international travel.

During this period a certain Muzungu by the names of Denis Hills was arrested by Amin for writing a book about a white pumpkin. I knew Ingrid Hills. I also gathered from Akiiki that a custodian at Livingstone

Hall had been whisked away by some guerrillas from Tanzania. Akiiki had been a resident of Livingstone Hall himself. My brother informed me through a third party that I should go into hiding following the havoc I had brought upon my sister. She had a miscarriage. Ten names appeared in the *Uganda Times* whose bearers were required to report to the Faculty of Education as having missed 4th term lectures. My name appeared twice on the same list for four days.

Now time approached for students destined for Moscow to depart. Scholarship winners from Uganda were to leave Entebbe in two batches, one week apart. Akiiki learned this information from Eliab who had been put on the first departees' list and whose brother was wedding that weekend. They both went together to the Soviet Embassy.

'Harasho. Tovarishi, harasho,' beamed the communist at Malcolm X avenue. Good comrades, he had said and had no objection. They exchanged tickets after the endorsement in Russian. I was to fly first, Eliab was happy to attend his brother's wedding and follow me to Moscow a week later on the same Aeroflot plane. In the confusion that ensued during the re-endorsement of visas, my names were mixed up so that the middle name came first and my Makerere surname of Tumusiime was abbreviated to Tussy. That way the henchmen's blacklist went begging.

I did not inform my brother about the change of my flight though we had agreed he would watch me board the plane from the waving bay. There was to be no physical contact whatsoever and I was at pains to write to him on an address in Kenya which he used to frequent. I was never to see him alive again having fallen victim of the notorious gang (from which he shielded me).

At the airport the then Uganda Broadcasting Corporation (BBC of Uganda as Amin called it) was airing a programme to the effect that Amin was willing to talk to Harold Wilson or Edward Heath (alternate British Premiers in the 70's) about the release of the British national Denis Hills. General Blair had been dismissed as a dranko. And to Russia, I flew past the red-eyed, red-topped vigilant and gallant soldiers. In the short run, I did come to love the Soviet Union and its peoples. I intend to publish and translate into Russian a series of short stories dedicated to comrade Baraire Barairevich Bararirev of which this one is the forerunner, Do savidaniya.

5
Sucked into the Barrel

Eng. N. Besigiroha

This time forget the usual wooden assembly of curved staves bound together by iron hoops for holding ale or beer, which is what a barrel is, but think of the other contrivances that man prefers to call barrels also. This particular barrel had a lot to do with Amin's Military Government.

Ever obsessed with consolidating its military might, the Government was at that time busy amassing a large arsenal of arms and other military equipment with the hub at Magamaga Ordinary Depot. Although the depot is located just above the railway station, there was no siding into the depot at the time. Since military cargo almost exclusively came in by rail, it was an inconvenience but most of all very sensitive security-wise having to carry the cargo to Jinja first, transshipping from rail to road trucks in the glare of the public eye, including hostile foreign ones, and returning the same cargo to the depot at Magamaga. It therefore made sense when the Government of the day decided that a siding be built from the railway station into the depot. Railway wagons would therefore be shunted into the depot untouched and offloaded or loaded at ease and in complete privacy. The only problems would be the technicalities involved owing to the topography between the depot and the railway station, directly below, and the time schedule demanded by the military.

The order came to railways for the siding to be put in place within a week, and if there were any problems they should be specified immediately and advised. When sent to investigate the site, I established that a siding would be possible but only just. Because of the big difference in level, the line would have to take a semi-circular detour at more than the normally permissible maximum curvature as a result stretching to about one kilometer in length. Even then, in order to obtain a negotiation gradient at reasonable load, the line would end in a cutting of about 2.5m deep. The next problem was the railways did not have any earth-moving equipment at all for the envisaged heavy excavations. The other problem was that the work was neither on the major nor minor works programme for the period. In other words, there were no funds for it. When these observations were passed on to the military authorities, the reaction was not reassuring although not unexpected either. Because it was specialised railway works, railways it was ruled, would do it at its own cost and be reimbursed later. Hopefully!

I reckoned we could fumble with the iron part of the work (the track) but I dared not risk the earthworks with borrowed and hired equipment. In the first instance practically nobody had such equipment and secondly in the event of delay or failure, the blame would obviously not be on the equipment hirer or lender. Having been through it once, I was anxious that everyone of us should be saved the possibility of having to do the now ritual disappearing acts (running into exile) or undergoing some other form of hardship or punishment should the work meet unexpected problems. I, therefore, convinced my superiors to insist on the army doing the earthworks since they could, I presumed, easily marshal or more correctly, commandeer, the necessary equipment; which, in fact, they rapidly did.

A Major Juma, a wiry hairlessold man from the Depot who obviously had not seen much school in his younger days, was assigned charge of the machinery, a traxcavator, D8 dozer and caterpillar grader and the responsibility of overseeing the construction. I am not sure whether he had ever seen combat action or ever supervised any engineering work but the way he beamed at me, this must have been the most important assignment he had ever had or the first one in a very long time. He enthused on how well he would do this 'kaji (kazi) kadogo' and show his bosses how efficient he was. It was obvious he probably, in spite of the title of Major, was one of the many supernumeraries around with no particular assignment and who was therefore always eager to please or impress, quite often very crudely and even brutally. He did not hide the fact that he expected big rewards at the end of the job. He immediately tried to engage me in the idle talk in his broken Kiswahili about his exploits during his younger days including those in 'Tanjania'. It would have been most entertaining had I time for it. Instead together with my surveyor we did a quick reconnaissance and returned to Kampala but before we left, Mzee Juma did not forget to remind me not to '*chelewesha kaji*' because to them everything was ready.

Back in Kampala, while we finalised the details of the scheme, I had the rails to worry about. I had earlier telephoned my Chief Engineer in Nairobi who fortunately happened to be a Ugandan from West Nile (Koboko in fact) and informed him about the crisis and how some rails had to be found somewhere in the system and sent over in double haste. Being from where I have said, he realised the implications if he did not act judiciously quickly and, on the other hand, the benefits there could be if he successfully executed a 'coup de maitre' in the affair. He, therefore, unilaterally used his powers to divert a consignment of secondhand rails that had been earmarked and loaded for another job on the Tanzania Tanga line. By the time the move was discovered, the consignment had crossed the border into Uganda. It almost cost him his job (we were then still one East African entity centrally governed), but this is another story.

The stir that this unauthorised act momentarily caused in Nairobi and Dar-es-Salaam would soon be settled through diplomatic gymnastics but for us in Kampala we had at least been relieved of a would-be major or even catastrophic hitch. We now braced ourselves. Amidst pressure from the Republic House we finalised the scheme and set out the alignment on the ground at Magamaga. We used conspicuous white markers on the double row of shoulder pegs only between which the excavation would be made. Then we walked Major Juma over the trace while I painstakingly explained what he had to do, emphasising how important it was to maintain the level indicating pegs which would control the depth of excavation. He once more enthused how easy all this was and how he had done it before, apparently the reason he had been specially chosen for it. He was to call us, or at least have us called, when he thought he was ready or in case he encountered any problem. He promptly boasted that unless he was let down by diesel supply, by the time we reached Kampala he would have called us back to inspect his finished work! I politely advised that he better wait to the morning for which we left him all agog. A twenty-four-hour liaison between Magamaga, Republic House and our office had been ordered.

He must have woken up early and literally set loose his machines because by early afternoon almost the whole of Magamaga hill had been stripped of all vegetation and almost flattened except for the fenced area of the depot. The narrow strip between the shoulder pegs marking the alignment and the levels or depth of excavation carefully indicated on special markers had apparently meant absolutely nothing to the Major. He had excavated as if preparing for Nambole Stadium. We did not learn of the tragedy from Major Juma's promised call to inspect the finished work, but through an SOS from the railway station late that evening to the effect the vital Kenya link had been breached and therefore closed.

As this was about the time of the aborted Tanzanian invasion (September 1972), the event immediately sparked off rumours of sabotage but what had happened was that late afternoon there had been a very heavy downpour. The resultant torrents heavily laden with the loose earth from Major Juma's handiwork cascaded down the hill with a potentially destructive force and had been only checked by the railway tracks below, which were promptly buried under the mountain of mud and slosh. It would take another day to clear the line and reopen it for traffic. Meanwhile, oblivious of the mess he had caused, Major Juma started sending incessant calls for inspection of his supposedly finished work very early next day. Fortunately that day the sun was bright and by the time I got to Magamaga mid afternoon, the breached railway line had already been cleared by the local track men. I, therefore, proceeded to inspect the siding work site which had been the cause of all the trouble. I could not believe what I saw of the excavation but this was, as destiny had it, not to be my immediate worry, or anybody else's for that matter.

I had carried the layout drawings of the proposed siding mainly to lay new strategy for the continuance of the work in the wake of Major Juma's havoc. We had been afforded a copy of the building layout inside the depot to facilitate design of the siding of the particular desired stores or armoury. This together with the staff car, a Peugeot 404, still bearing the famous oval maroon EARC logo were to be my undoing. We drove up a side track that ran parallel and close to the depot fence to the point where I estimated the siding would be entering from. Since the setting out pegs were no more, I got out of the car and began the inspection with the rolled drawing in my hand for case of reference. Looking up the hill through the 2 mesh fence I noticed a group of three or four soldiers sitting under a large tree, presumably mango, about 70-100m away inside the depot. There were one or two jerrycans nearby and the soldiers were holding containers that looked like tumblers. They were most likely on a waragi binge.

Missed, however, had been one other soldier, a tall dark figure who was sauntering down the hill towards where I was at the fence. 'Simama! Kuja,' he ordered as he quickened his pace. A little unnerved but not suspecting much trouble I stepped up and shortly we came face to face, only separated by the wire mesh of the fence. 'Wewe nani na onafanya nini?' (Who are you and what are you doing?). He was clearly suspicious when I explained that I was a railway official supervising the construction of the proposed siding into the depot. How would I know there was supposed to be such work since I was a civilian, he wondered, pacing menacingly, a little to the left and then to the right. 'Toa density' he finally ordered meaning I should identify myself by producing my 'Identity Card'.

The fence was over 2m high and the card was rather too big to go through the mesh so I did what I thought was the most sensible and practical thing to do. I opened up the card in my palm and held it against the fence for him to read. As if stung by a bee, he flinched back a couple of steps and declared the card was too far for him to read, if he could read, that is. I began to feel rather nervous, sweaty and awkward. For some inexplicable reason he was getting agitated. As I fumbled he ordered,' Tupa iyo density'. Throw away my identity card? How ridiculous! 'But ...' I began to plead, but I neither could find the right words nor finish the sentence because he quickly shifted his gun pointing it at me and ordering that I toss the card over the fence to him. Realising my very weak position I did as told but began to wonder and fear how I would be able to go back to Kampala through the numerous and often impromptu check points without identification should my tormentor decide not to give it back.

He picked up the card and demanded to know my name although for all I know he might have been holding the card upside down. Then tragedy struck! The designer of the card had apparently not sufficiently taken into consideration the long names of the West because my first and second names spread over two lines on the card like a sentence, with hardly any space in between them. So when I declared my second name which begins with a 'B' it certainly did not sound like what appeared on the card, where the 'sentence' began with an 'N' the initial of the first name. The soldier triumphantly nodded to himself, gymnastically reasoning, *'Kumbe ni kweli gorira iko hapa'* (so it is true there are guerrillas around).

From his naïve misreading of the identity card or merely out of caprice he had concluded that the card was a stolen one and obviously not mine in spite of a clear photograph of me. I was therefore a wrong element and he loudly declared so in no uncertain terms. I was beginning to plead once again when he pointed at the roll of drawings in my hand which was now quivering uncontrollably and demanded to know what the *'karatasi'* was. I committed my biggest blunder. I opened the drawings and naively overrating his capacity to discern such matters, tried to explain how it was intended to construct a siding into the depot, pointing out the route and the other physical features on the map. That I knew what each of the little squares and circles represented sealed my fate. I must be a super spy who not only knew the sensitive depot in and out but had managed to map it obviously for the benefit of the now known external invasion. This was, in his thinking, confirmed beyond any doubt when he chanced to look across to where my car was and noticed it had foreign numbers (the car had recently been transferred to us from Kenya) and what he decided was a secret logo. All hell broke loose. He unslung his gun and held it at the ready declaring what a lucky man he was. That night he boasted he would celebrate with the biggest shots, his bosses, and be suitably rewarded for being the first one to capture and actually kill a *'gorira.'* *'Na uwa gorira sasa hivi, kabisa,* (I am killing a guerrilla now).

My driver Erisa, getting concerned about the goings on came out of the car to add his pleas to mine which had been of no consequence. The soldier's wrath immediately turned on him. There was suddenly a cracking noise that in my inexperienced and frightened state sounded very much like a shot but which apparently was only the gun cocking.

Erisa was ordered to get back into his car and drive away, never looking back, until he reported to whoever had sent us and brought him back to the disposed of just like I was about to be. Erisa's shock and therefore momentary hesitation prompted another crack which sent me into a final stupor.

'*Sasa wewe sema u gorira*' (Now confess that you are a guerrilla) I heard the words and many more urging me not to waste anymore of his time. '*Sema*' he shouted, each time more menacingly. I must have tried to speak but there was a heavy choking lump in my throat and no sound came out. Better it did not, because I would have hated condemning myself in my fright. It had been quite a while now, for me an eternity, and the other group under the mango tree must have began wondering what was going on because one of them rose up and began coming down at the same time calling 'Nini hapo?' To me I was only imagining or hallucinating about this movement and sound but they were both apparently real.

My adversary, who was irked by the intrusion and obviously anxious and intent on getting his prize trophy before anybody interfered, shouted back that there was a guerrilla whom he was proceeding to kill immediately. '*Ngoja*' (wait) the other man shouted as he increased his pace which infuriated the goon the more. I may have been only imagining but I saw him take definite aim and I could not dare look any more. I instinctively threw up my arms above my head, the drawings involuntarily dropping out of my hands, and earnestly prayed that he would shoot. I had had enough fright to care any more and a quick end might be better in the circumstances.

When we were very young, at one time or another and in some cases frequently, we used to dream about falling into a bottomless pit. Although only a dream, it used to be a harrowing experience with a characteristic sensation. Our mothers, aunties and older siblings used to interpret the dream as growing up. It was believed the gravitational pull during the endless fall stretched your limbs and that is how you grew taller. Mine was now a different kind of sensation. I had all this while been looking straight into this very small dark hole hardly big enough to swallow an ordinary bic pen (the barrel of the menacing gun) but now I suddenly felt a painless thump of some pointed object onto my chest which I imagined was a bullet entering my body and I became oblivious of everything around me, audio or visual, except for this little hole which began to rapidly grow larger with multicolored concentric rings radiating from it and themselves growing larger and yet larger in the kaleidoscope like the computer graphics you now frequently see on TV and computer game screens. In a desperate but futile struggle I was quickly being sucked towards the black spot, the faraway end and vanishing point of the conical cylinder along which I was now gliding. Eternity?

I do not know how long this went on but my dream was suddenly interrupted by some voices. It seems at some point I had blacked out but I opened my eyes and became aware of my surroundings. At the same time tears must have welled up in my eyes in torrents which played havoc to my vision. Where there had been the single tormentor there now at first seemed to be a rather burly man, was having a bitter argument with the rogue.

He seemed more disciplined and must have at least been of a higher rank for my hitherto tormentor was now rather subdued and no longer in control in spite of his continued protestations that I must be either a guerrilla or at least an agent who must be killed.

The newcomer who qualifies to have been my saviour had now secured my identity card and having studied it interrogated me afresh. To him my explanation made sense and he confirmed for the benefit of his colleague and stubbornly insisted on ignorance of the scheme, that there was indeed a siding planned for them and Major Juma was in charge. This notwithstanding, the rogue vehemently protested at how a proven guerrilla was being let off and how he was being denied his would-be reward and possible promotion. Next time, he vowed, he would shoot at sight. In a way, he had a point crooked as it may have been, because at that dark once dead anybody could have qualified for a guerrilla and a reason for a reward.

I have never known and I will never know who my savior was but I got back my ID (tossed over the fence again). I hurried away never to come back to Magamaga. Although I could have easily got one in the back, I never waited to ask for a dismissal.

Just before the station, Erisa gave me a terrible fright when he crawled out of the bush and welcomed me with an almost inaudible *'Kulikayo Ssebo'*. I was so taken aback but sincerely touched by his loyalty when I recovered. He had greatly risked his own life by sticking around. He had stealthily parked the car behind a bush further down the hill, he said, and crawled back on his belly under cover of the bush to a vantage point from where he had watched in absolute horror what had ensued. Quite obviously his brave act had been not to save me for there was no way he could have saved me but, had the inevitable happened, he had wished to carry the correct story especially to my family as the official version would obviously have been that an engineer had been collaborating with the guerrillas or had simply run away, which was the common explanation for the numerous disappearances of the day. Each of us must have been having his own reflections on the incident during the drive back to Kampala. We drove in absolute silence.

    We got back to Kampala soon after dusk and I went straight to my house where I telephoned the then Regional Manager and told him that I would under no circumstances go back to Magamaga and I was in any case resigning my job. He did not understand and indeed he could not understand because in spite of his entreaties, I did not give him the benefit of an explanation of what had happened, as I was still in a lugubrious state. Moreover, you were never sure whether such matters should be reported for fear of the possible consequences depending on where the report finally landed. Nonetheless he must have sensed that something had gone terribly wrong at Magamaga and acted quickly because the next morning while I still mused over my intended resignation, I was summoned to Republic House by no other than the Minister of Defence, respectable late Oboth Ofumbi.

6
Bomb Disposal Expert
Eng. N. Besigiroha

The liberation war was already raging around Lukaya and Lwera. A few of Amin's aircraft had been downed, tanks had begun to litter the roads and some of the unfortunate Libyan mercenaries had been killed and their bodies were being secretly shipped back to Tripoli. The country and particularly the military government was on tension while the majority of the civilians prayed for the advance on Kampala to accelerate not only the end of the war but also that of the tyrannical regime.

The Uganda National Liberation Army (UNLA) had devised a number of ingenious tactics. Of late they were attacking major or strategic installations, especially power pylons and railway bridges. Railway bridges were very useful targets because their demobilisation effectively slowed down supplies to Amin's troops. The strategy, I learnt later, was not to destroy the structures which the elite UNLA strategists very well knew were so vital for rebuilding the economy if the war succeeded, but to inflict at least some damage to divert the government troops from the actual fighting to the impossible task of guarding the innumerable vulnerable structures and other facilities scattered all over the country. It was an effective strategy because hundreds of government troops were effectively demobilised in this manner. However, one pitied those whose responsibility included management of or actual repair of the damaged structures of the above category. You lost either way. If you did not effect the repairs you would be labelled a saboteur and whenever you effected the repairs often under armed guard or at gun point, the liberators, if they knew you personally and their spy network was superb, would send you messages warning you of frustrating the war effort. This used to be a very uncomfortable situation imagining what might befall you, if they eventually succeeded in taking over.

I had recently returned from one such mission at a bridge in Mukono District where we had spent two days with a Minister on repair work when I was called upon or more correctly forced to execute another impossible task. By this time all the major railway and road bridges, electrical power substations and many other installations were under 24-hour armed guard. The road-over-rail bridge on Masaka Road just off Mityana Road roundabout popularly known as Katooga was therefore no exception.

I had just dropped my young daughter at Buganda Road Primary School and proceeded to the office on what began as a normal day but which later turned into a nightmare or the longest day just like a John Wayne epic World War II film. As I parked my car I was promptly approached by three ruggedly dressed, armed, as usual, junior looking soldiers who wished to know whether I was 'the railway engineer.' There was very little or no alternative to saying I was, knowing that trying to clarify my rank whether Regional, District or Assistant Engineer would only have been rigmarole for them. In that case, there was an assignment for me and because they had no transport my car would be used for the assignment. My official driver had not yet reported or may have actually already been upstairs at my office but I was given no chance to pick him because as they said, although without explaining the nature of the mission, it was a matter of life and death. As a matter of fact they took offence that I had come so late; when it was only 8.30 am, so monstrously early for a typical Ugandan, in the middle of a war especially if he had the burden of dropping a wife or child on the way. Two of the soldiers were already impatiently tugging at the car door handles.

I took the wheel and drove out of the gates. You would excuse some of my colleagues who were now beginning to trickle in who looked on rather worriedly. Driving away with three unknown soldiers without the official driver had a lot of negative connotations and not unnatural for the period, therefore speculation and rumour started to circulate as the day wore on because I did not return. Our destination was Katoogo, Masaka Road. When around Katwe, I was told the problem was a bomb that had apparently been placed under the bridge on the railway line. I attempted to turn back because the way it was, I tried to explain, I was the wrong person for the exercise. This almost earned me a beating. Apparently the gentlemen, if I may call them that, had never heard of a bomb-disposal unit in their own army and in any case even if there was somebody like a disposal expert this, to them, was different. The bomb was on the railway and since an outside bomb expert would most likely tamper with the railway line while attempting to defuse the bomb, it must be the railway engineer who knows how to protect the railway track, who should handle the bomb. The way it was, if the bomb had been planted in a hotel kitchen it would be the hotel chef to handle it or if in a hospital, the doctor. Fantastic reasoning or how marvellously stupid!

At the bridge, we got out of the car and I was only allowed to go halfway down the embankment (for fear of the bomb going off in spite of my supposed expertise). I peered at a small mount of earth in the middle of the railway tract directly under the bridge which the soldiers pointed out to be the suspected bomb. It had apparently been spotted by one of their patrol about six o'clock that morning. In normal circumstances one would have crucified these soldiers for not promptly reporting such a potentially serious matter to their bosses instead of walking all the way to railways. But that is the type of people they were.

Anyway, now that I had seen what they suspected, what did I have to say.

From where we were, I observed that a mount of what appeared to be fresh earth had been made around one of the metal center-line pegs normally used to keep perfect alignment of the railway tracks under bridges. It was that metal peg that had convinced the soldiers that it was in fact a detonating device. My verdict was that someone had obviously played with the peg but for there being a bomb I could not tell. It might as well have been children previously grazing cows or goats there but since I did not want to take chances I advised that the matter be reported to the bomb disposal unit for more expert investigation, emphasising that time was of essence if it was indeed a bomb.

Everybody seemed to agree. We therefore got back to the car and drove to Makindye barracks, my idea of reporting to Republic House instead being pushed aside. Badly irritating too, was the fact that although the soldiers seemingly believed in and were much concerned about the bomb, they rejected my pleas to go to the railway control office and ensure that no trains were ignorantly dispatched from Kampala or Bujuko into the section. The horror of a passenger train possibly being blown up, which in any case must have been the bomb planter's aim, if he existed that is, did not seem to worry them as much as they worried about their bosses.

The discussion in the car was 'suppose we find Captain or Major so and so? Don't you think he will be mad at us?' Mad for what, I wondered, when a catastrophe was looming.

At the barracks, we reported to a Sergeant Major's guard office, but he was not there. I asked if there was anybody more senior and I was rudely told to mind my own business and let the military protocol take its own course. The remarks notwithstanding, I was getting impatient at the general attitude. If it was a landmine it would be triggered if a train attempted to pass and equally if it was a time bomb it would not sit there all day unless the planters had no purpose. I tried to put these arguments across as we drove back to Katoogo with the Sergeant Major, who, when he came and received the report, *(kuna bomb kwa daraja na inginia ameona)*, he had decided to go and see for himself. At least he saw the point and on the way allowed me to alert the traffic control office to stop the trains. Fortunately, they were not many, the one from Kampala only due in the evening.

Immediately after he saw the suspect spot the Sergeant Major declared, *'Kweli hi ni bomb? Nilazima tuwa eleze wakubwa'* (For sure this is a bomb. We must inform the bosses). Back to Makindye! I had never seen such callousness. The Sergeant Major wished to report to the Lieutenant. What followed was simply ridiculous and dreadful. The Lieutenant was also not around and nothing could therefore be done. Could I be released because I had other things to do and in any case there was nothing more I could help? No. I had been witness and being the expert (merely by virtue of being an engineer) I was the right person to report the matter to the 'wakubwa'. It was now past 11 o'clock and I was really getting frustrated.

Meanwhile, in the idleness that followed, gossip about the bomb went around and all the idle soldiers gathered to discuss it, if all the nonsensical comments and ideas put forward could be termed discussion. On my part I took a little while off to take in the geography of the place. The buildings, all barrack type, were arranged around a quadrangle with the office block along one of the longer sides. This building had a polished saucer-shaped plinth that seemed to slope to the far end where a papyrus mat screen shielded a lower level. Somebody sat on a chair slightly behind the screen with a heavy whip, and so motionless he could have been mistaken for a statue. Although I was not in here for any mischief, it was frightening enough merely to be there from the stories one used to hear about these particular barracks.

My study was interrupted when at long last the metal gate clanged open and what I learnt a while later to be the Lieutenant sauntered in, in macabre style. He wore a rough turtleneck under his military fatigues and was really menacing to look at. He had a short cane in one hand and was holding a young short man by the scruff of his neck and roughly shoving him ahead of him and kicking. He was throwing all sorts of obscenities at the poor whimpering wretch. Everybody else went dead silent.

Halfway along the office verandah the Lieutenant gave the unfortunate young man a very heavy push together with a bone-cracking kick that sent him hurting and slithering along the apron towards the statue-like form at the papyrus screen. The accompanying order 'Kimbia' should not have really been necessary. At the other end, the statue casually lifted a boot over which the young man tripped and fell down the lower level. The hitherto idle figure sprang into action like a leopard, jumping in after the young man. Although hidden by the screen what followed was unmistakable. The man was being treated to a savage beating. What started off as heart rendering shrieks and screams gradually waned to groans and grunts, then whimpers and finally to silence. The torturer then jumped out of the pit and gleefully reported to his master that it was unlikely the fellow would dare to be cheeky again. Halfway through the drama, I had touched the Sergeant Major's sleeve and reminded him of the bomb but he had said, *'goja mukubwa amalize hi kitu kwanza'*. This was madness at its worst. The Lieutenant was meanwhile raucously but obviously happily narrating the story of the young man. He was apparently a mechanic whose sister was a concubine (willing or most likely forced) of the Lieutenant. The young man had been repairing the soldier's car for months on end without getting paid. Today he had been cheeky enough, according to the Lieutenant, not only to ask for payment for previous bills but to refuse to repair the car this time. Using the most vulgar and obscene words that cannot possibly be repeated here, the man castigated his victim for thinking that having his sister as a concubine would protect him from his wrath or give him a ticket to insolence. I had never experienced such sadism.

It was after he had told all the latest dirty stories he had recently been involved in that he inquired about the latest events at the station. It is then that we finally reverted to the bomb and, as if it had all been rehearsed, the Lieutenant also wanted to see for himself before doing anything. It was getting to 1.00 pm but my request to pick my little girl from school and to try and get a driver received the harshest of responses. I was now on emergency national duty I was told and my child or family did not matter at all. I was reminded soldiers were dying at the hands of the rebels, so who was minding their children? So back to Katoogo. At Katwe we ran out of fuel. We turned into Katwe Roundabout petrol station and were served but drove out without paying. I, however, do not think the attendant had accountability problems later because very soon after, the war reached Kampala and everybody started to run. At Katoogo the Lieutenant also asserted that there was a bomb. He ordered for reinforcements to cordon off the area for a radius of about 100m. We must have been lucky to have such a patient and considerate bomb that seemed to fully take into consideration the general ignorance and inefficiency in the soldiery.

We must once more report to the 'wakubwa' and back to Makindye it was. Because of the nature of my company and from what I had seen happen to the unfortunate young mechanic a little back, I decided I should not offer any more stupid suggestions and merely concentrated on being an obedient chauffeur, the deep concern about my now hungry and possibly crying little girl at school and many other worries notwithstanding. A rumour was already circulating around the office about my having been taken in the then common parlance.

This time round we were a little luckier. A major (not a captain) was at station when we arrived! Not only this, he appeared a bit more understanding and spoke some reasonable English. He, however, also suffered from the common disease of wanting to see before believing but his demeanour put me back to ease and I eventually was able to bring up the subject of the army bomb disposal unit as we drove back to Katoogo, for the fourth time now. Most unbelievably, he also did not seem too certain about the unit and opined that in any case they would most likely now all be at the war front at Lukaya. He was however quick at deciding to report the matter to Republic House which is what everyone before him should have done in the first instance.

Republic House was a hive of activity especially in the control (radio) room where Amin's own voice could be heard presumably giving orders to his commanders at the front from above the crackle and static of the radio. The atmosphere was extremely tense and the soldiers, immediately when they heard what was going on the radio disappeared, I presume to the control room, abandoning me in the waiting room. From what I could piece together from the cacophony of radios and the soldier's voices, a plane or two had just been shot down, there had been a number of casualties and everything was certainly not going well at the war front.

It was then that Major General Emilio Mondo stepped into the waiting room in combat fatigues. Everybody else I had seen so far had been equally battle ready. He was flustered as to what a civilian was doing in there at such a sensitive moment. I recognised him from our University days in Nairobi in the early sixties and when I stood up to give him respect he also recognised me. When I hurriedly explained what the problem was he sighed in resignation. 'No wonder the war is being lost if we are continuing to behave like this!' It was obvious from his reaction that this was not the first or the only mess up since the war started.

He immediately sprang into action making a number of frantic telephone calls from a neighboring room. In his last call I could hear him giving directions and instructions to the person at the end of the line. Shortly after, he stepped back into the room. He thanked me and said that a bomb disposal car was on the way. You should have seen the faces of the Major and his group when they reappeared only to find the Major General had already taken control of the serious matter and that what they had come to report had not been done promptly.

Soon after, a pitch black Peugeot arrived with a single occupant. The Major General instructed that since I had been at it all day I should see it through to the end. I, together with my group, accompanied the disposal car back to the site. At a safe distance from the bridge where we were directed by the disposal expert, we watched as he directed and redirected probes from the boot laboratory of the car. When apparently nothing dangerous was detected he went down the bank with more gadgets to the suspect spot where more superficial investigations were made. I held my breath as the expert put aside his gadgets and started digging around the peg, carefully checking and rechecking his instruments as he dug deeper and deeper until he uprooted the metal peg completely. He dug a little more, reached hard ground and was satisfied that nothing was buried there. He came back up, repacked his equipment and declared that the whole thing had been a hoax but expressed gratitude that he had been called, (although I am not sure he knew that the whole thing had been so bungled it could have been too late) emphasising that however remotely suspicious anything looked it must not be taken for granted in the then prevailing situation.

We reported the results to Republic House before I hurried, as if hurrying would save anything now, to check on my child. I was terribly exhausted having had no lunch or refreshment of any kind but the poor girl had suffered a lot more. She had cried herself hoarse when I failed to pick her up. She had also not eaten and her class and playmates had long gone and the agony of seeing some of them picked by their parents had been too much for her. She was the lone figure at the verandah as dusk gathered. It was 6.45 pm. Ironically, the next morning I was ostracised by the school authorities for negligence and child abuse.

Just like John Wayne's, it was the longest day.

7
Dilemma in Dicey Situations 1979
George Akol

The front line of the liberators, *wakombozi* as they were popularly known at the time, 1979, had by first week of April reached Budo, 18km West of Kampala. There was obvious panic in the city and the country at large. It became imperative for Amin's government to close offices early so as to give time for workers to reach their respective homes before dark. Offices were to close at 4.00 pm and general curfew was imposed in the entire country from 6.00 pm to 6.00 am. The general security in Uganda was placed in the hands of key ministries and military personnel. The set-up was headed and chaired by a colonel.

It is against that background that the writer, an engineering officer in the city, was drawn into providing security facilitation for what was 'for planning security of the city.' One such incident difficult to deal with was to comply with the directive from the top security meeting to have all street lights switched off in under one hour. I had to confirm this instruction before complying with it. Did it indeed come from the very top security body? At the time it was quite possible to settle personal vendettas by tricking a colleague into falsehoods.

Anyhow, I telephoned Uganda Electricity Board (UEB), with whom we had a working relationship as customer/supplier, on the instruction to disconnect power to street lights. The UEB engineer barked over the telephone that his Minister of Energy had given instruction to the contrary. He had also been tensed up. I told him I reserved the rights, as the lighting authority in the city to give final decision whether lights be on or off. I rang off and then followed up to establish the position with the Minister of Local Government. Protocol in a normal government is such that to contact a minister on official matters it would be through the Permanent Secretary. This I did. The response from the Permanent Secretary was daunting. There was a palpable difference that caused one rift between the two persons. I was told rudely to 'talk to your Minister'. So I did ring the Minister's office in the event of his late working. No response. I tried the house, much the same – no response.

After several unsuccessful attempts, what next? I decided to telephone the very top of the security meeting, that is the colonel.

I had never been in official contact with military personnel at any level that mattered, with exception of relatives of course. The apathy originated from early school days when problem students, be it for rudeness, drunkenness, indiscipline or superannuation, were dismissed only to turn up as uniformed soldiers! With a mind like that I had to talk to a soldiering boss whose command of the English language was suspect. An alternative was to be equipped with Swahili at above '*duka wallah*' standard of the forties up to the seventies. The army office switchboard response was easy to handle. In cheap Swahili I said *mimi nataka Bwana* Colonel. *Wewe nani*? Was enquiry as to whom I was. *mimi Engineer ya taa* was my response concerning street lighting. After some moments, the switchboard fellows said '*Bwana iko kwa Parliament.* '*Goja,*' meaning wait. The next response was an operator in Parliamentary building. This time the response was in English 'Do you want Chairman of the Security Council?' I replied in the affirmative. 'Hold on,' the operator said.

After a minute another operator, this time in Uganda Club, asked who I was. I told him who I was and who I'd wanted to speak to and there he was! In the meanwhile I looked at my watch and had only 15 minutes to confirm time. Being rather apprehensive as to what language the Colonel was to speak, I introduced myself in beginner's expression in English so as to be understood right away. The Colonel's spoken English turned out to be above average. He had said that the issue of street lighting had come up in their agenda for the day and that they had to be on. With that hurdle having been sorted out, what now, of my Minister's contrary view point?

After drawing blanks in trying to contact the Minister again, I jumped into my car a few minutes to the start of the curfew hour, crossed form Kololo to Mbuya Hill where the Minister's agent used to reside. The agent was the one who had sent me the written instruction as having emanated from the Minister. After 6.00 pm nearly every homestead gate was bolted and absolute silence regained. Radios were snuffled, especially those turned to foreign stations that were said to malign the military government. So there was no reply to banging the gate! I drove back dreading to meet any obstacle. I didn't meet even a dog all the way. Clearly audible were gun shots all over the place. As to where they were directed, I do not know but I did survive to tell this story.

It wasn't long after that incident that the *Wakombozi* surrounded the city. General looting by fleeing Amin's soldiers had picked up momentum. After one of my employer's trucks had been hijacked, I gave instruction to the transport office to have vehicle keys to be under my custody and fuel injectors in the engines were to be removed from all trucks except garbage trucks which would be unattractive to the looters – so I thought!

When I received a telephone call at the house that a garbage truck had been hijacked, I immediately telephoned the Kampala District Police Commander about the theft. He told me 'let them take, engineer. You are in fact disturbing my packing. I am on my way upcountry right now. It was then that I realised that there was no longer a government in the country. Failure of policing was a clear indicator that there was no peace in the country and that law and order had collapsed.

Overnight I also planned to depart. The question was with what vehicle? I had a rather unsound personal car but then there was no fuel to be obtained anywhere. The only option was to go with one of the office tippers for which emergency fuel was in drums. A large part of my family had actually gone upcountry about a month earlier, except for two. My son and daughter had to brave attending school despite intermittent running home in response to grenade bursts and gunshots. My plan at the time was to have a colonel brother-in-law take my children to their mother and that I would seek refuge with a friend at Makerere University pending success or failure of the *Wakombozi*. In any cast it was not safe for the escape to an area where Amin was still in authority. I would be regarded as an enemy sympathiser. So, now the in-law was to collect my children from a neighbour at 8.00 am on the critical morning following the Police Commander's departure.

The 8.00 am appointment flopped. The colonel had departed half an hour earlier. The hour of change of plans had come, I then drove my ramshackle car with my children in uniform, along Kitante Road to 6th Street where the transport fleet was kept. All along Kiira Road to 6th Street were haggard-looking armed soldiers flanking either side of the street. Depressed chugging alongside them. With me were the bunch of truck keys. I was now determined to go upcountry with my children, the ones I would not risk sending home alone with a driver. On reaching the transport office, I picked one tipper that had a sure performance record with its somewhat abrasive driver suitable to match any crude situation that could arise. The tipper was driven to the service pit to load the fuel drum. In the meanwhile, two armed soldiers marched through the main gate manhandling one of our drivers towards where I was. It was a transport truck they had wanted to run off with, to West Nile. I made a deliberate lie to save the driver that I did not have a driver. They retorted saying that they had seen the fellows driving a refuse truck near the barracks, if I didn't know that. *'Shauri yako'*, i.e. Sorry for you! I shrugged my shoulders and told them to pick a truck of their choice. Silly thing was I had placed the bunch of keys on my cabinet. All the same I still had the catch of fuel jets having been removed from the vehicles to incapacitate engine firing. As soon as the soldiers went for their pick I sent someone scurrying to tell my intended driver to rush out of the depot with the tipper to my house in the event of soldiers turning their attention to my tipper. In point of fact they did! Hard luck it was for them. I bade my staff good-bye and left the soldiers to their fate. I learnt three months later from the driver that they did take him but on another hijacked tipper found on the highway.

I drove off with my children from the depot at about 11.00 am. On reaching Kitante Road and driving towards Mulago, right ahead of me at the Golf Club could be seen an entire dual carriage way and the roundabout packed with soldiers in an apparent regrouping. I swung the car up on detour along Shimoni Road, All Saints Church, Nakasero Hill down to Kitante Road once again. You can believe it, all along this time there were no cars on the road. On reaching the house I was relieved to find my tipper ready and moderately packed with personal effects. The driver had already picked his family to flee with me. I abandoned my car at the residence of the police boss whom I had mentioned previously. He had fled ahead of me!

We left at once trying to beat the 6.00pm curfew hour at the end to the 300km journey east wards from Kampala. We had, however, to get back to the depot for the fuel drum, the loading of which was interrupted by intruding soldiers.

The tipper backed to the service pit so that the drum be pushed on. While this was being done, we suddenly heard the whizzing of a bomb over head. We couldn't see where it was. Could we have been sighted by long range guns as one of the few vehicles moving at the time? A few seconds later the bomb exploded and we sighed with relief that it was not anywhere near where we were. It was later known to have fallen by the railway station 300m away.

We drove off from the depot in trepidation and our fears were immediately realised because just by the Kitante roundabout lay the body of a man, dressed in a suit, suitcase by his side, but split wide open at the bowels! This was a shocking experience for my 10- and 8-year-olds sitting beside me. Getting just past this spot were broken window panes of the shops alongside Kitante Road. These breakages and the manner of slaughtering of the dead man were said to be typical of the 'Saba Saba' long-range bombs which explode while belching out sharp blades that shear through anything.

We now headed towards Jinja, all in silence and appreciating every inch distancing us from such bombs. At the Ntinda Road turnoff, shortly after Nakawa Market, the road was reduced to a single lane by mass of soldiers waving down any moving vehicle eastwards to stop. It wasn't an official road checkpoint but the soldiers had wanted lifts away from the front line which had closed in at Natete and Makerere in the west, Katwe and Makindye in the south. I instructed the driver to halt and that from then I would not speak to any intruders. This was for fear of being softspoken and therefore malleable to soldierly arm twisting by whoever was the commander among these soldiers and who was demanding for lifts for soldiers going our way. My driver said we were going to Soroti to escort the boss, meaning myself, as it was permitted by Amin for persons to dispatch their families home and then come back to fight. About a platoon that was armed with AK rifles jumped to the back of the tipper. Two of these soldiers with their guns forced their way to the cabin dislodging my children to the back of the tipper. I kept mum, pulling my cap further down my face to hide the anger welling in my chest and my eyes getting bloodshot.

We then set off and it must have been about 1km. Either side of the carriage way to Jinja was a pathetic scene of trekking as far as one's feet could go; Hardly any motorised traffic anywhere; mothers and fathers carrying kids on their backs. Personal effects appeared to have been left behind to whosoever was concerned. It was stinking in the cabin with bad breath and body odour from the intruders. I later learnt that the soldiers had not had a wash for three months. They had been in the 'New Uganda District' of Kagera in Tanzania as occupied by Amin's army in early stages of the war. Their side of the story was of a narrow escape after having been besieged at Uganda-Tanzania border by the *Wakombozi*.

We had all been silent for about half an hour. Then one soldier abruptly asked if I could drive a car. I said I did. He then instructed my driver that if he sights a good car in any direction he should wave for him to be chauffeur driven home! Another of his demands after a while, was that the property at the back of the tipper was no longer mine but from then on it belonged to him.

Any nice looking girls could also be kidnapped for his sake! The tipper rolled on but had to turn off to Nabisunsa Girls Secondary School. A colleague outside the country had requested me to collect his daughter to drop at his house in Mbale. On reaching the school gate, the girls on seeing soldiers perched at the back of the tipper went flying criss-crossing the school compound to wherever they considered secure. I jumped off the cabin walking majestically to give the impression of confidence and no cause for panic to the European headmistress' office. She, however, showed no feeling of uneasiness. With a few select words of assurance to her, she granted the release of the girl. Also the knowing look of the girl on seeing me did help to ease the atmosphere.

We set off again to the main road till Njeru town opposite the Nile Beer Brewery, where a strongly manned road block was set up and every soldier was ordered off the truck except civilians, an unusual practice. All the soldiers were disarmed including my cabin mates. Did they look for bombs without guns? Absolutely subdued they looked, giving me a feeling of being somewhat secure. The looting soldier now felt more homesick than concerned about property. He looked forward to getting off at old Busia road and going to his abode.

Getting past Owen Falls Dam, we turned to Butiki Secondary School to pick up a friend's son. With *saba-saba* guns now 80km away, these diversions now gave concern for delaying to beat curfew hour. At the Busia Trading Center the marauding soldier jumped off without a fuss. The girl did the same in Mbale. On getting to the outskirts of Mbale, another army group of about eight soldiers stepped on our vehicle urging us to drop them at Soroti. My driver told them that it was close to curfew time and the only help we could give them was only to Kumi. So they jumped on the truck. On reaching the main junction on entering Kumi, I told the driver to stop and ordered the soldiers in the cabin with us to see to the disembarking of all the soldiers. While they were disembarking, I overheard one of the soldiers beginning to stir up trouble. He said that truck was a government vehicle and that it could be commanded anywhere even up to Soroti. I immediately shouted to my 'new bodyguard' soldier to jump on and we let fly. This he did, I instructed the driver to take a diversionary course lest these soldiers could track us on foot. My home was then nine km from the junction. We weaved our way over grassy ground to leave no trail until we reached home to a tearful reception just after the start of the curfew hour.

8
Living with Death

Peace Anguzu

On 10th October 1976, at National Sugar Works Kinyara Limited (NSWL), Masindi, a group of about ten of us continued to celebrate Independence Day. Around 11.00 am, one Joseph Kwizera, a Munyarwanda and a construction overseer with Africonstra, came to join us. He was a very arrogant fellow and because of this, had created many enemies including some people in our group. He had come indecently dressed in ill-fitting shorts. His t-shirt was wrinkled and very offending to us. Kwizera was told in no uncertain language that he was abusing our independence as well as being idle and disorderly; that if he was to stay with us he had to change his dress or face the risk of our burning the T-shirt. We agreed to pay him five times the cost of the t-shirt if it came to burning the t-shirt which cost three shillings at that time. Kwizera was also broke. At the prospect of 15 shillings, he simply peeled off the T-shirt and handed it to us. Within 15 minutes the t-shirt was ashes and Kwizera was paid his 15 shillings.

At the time, Captain Charles Ziraba was the Security Officer at NSWL Kinyara. He was a Musoga and allegedly related to Mama Mariam Amin. This man had become intolerable in the army and had been expelled. Being a 'Muko' of Big Daddy, the man found himself in Kinyara where he also doubled as a State Research Bureau agent. He was very much responsible for the terror that existed in Kinyara, in factory, the man had all records of day, time and minute when say a fuse blew somewhere, or a boiler tripped. These were, according to him and his masters, acts of sabotage against the government. The man was practically hated by everyone. It was to this Ziraba that Kwizera, in a bid to amend relations between them and armed with our 15 shillings, reported over drinks that afternoon of 10th October 1976 that we had burnt the PORTRAIT of the President. With this stunning revelation Captain Ziraba directly reported us to the military with a recommendation that we be arrested immediately.

Rumours of our impending arrest were already circulating on the morning of 11th October 1976. The rest of our group who had heard of our impending arrests fled. Unfortunately on the 10th, Onega Luciano and I had slept at a nearby trading center, having over-enjoyed ourselves. We had not heard. Around 10.00 am, a Peugeot 304 driven by a plain-clothed soldier came looking for us at the trading center. He was accompanied by one company security guard. The guard said that the government agent, then Genero Charles Olok (now RIP) wanted to see us. We were still ignorant. We did not know how the third man, Otto, a mechanic was picked. Charles Kamugisha, a cashier, was arrested from his office. This is how the four of us were arrested. Little did we know that matters had taken a more serious course. We did not even know that a military Land Rover with four armed men was parked out of sight behind the Government Agent's Office.

At the G/A's office we were informed of the crime we had committed against the state – TREASON. Our argument that the t-shirt we burnt did not bear any portrait of the President was waved down. The Sergeant in the G/A's office then said we had to give statements at Masindi Police Station. He also promised the G/A that we would be returned later in the day. As we came out, the area around the office was cordoned off and Charles Kamugisha, Luciano Onega, Otto, Joseph Kwizera and myself were escorted to Masindi Police Station in the afternoon. We were not returned as promised to the G/A. We did not make statements because according to the police, our case was beyond their jurisdiction. We spent the night there and were whisked off to the army Barracks quarter-guard house at 9.00 am the next morning.

The Ag. C/O Masindi at that time was Major Saidi Abiriga. That week over fifty military top brass countrywide were at a signals communication course in Masindi. When we arrived at the quarter-guard we were told that the C/O would interview us at the officers' Mess at 2.00 pm that afternoon. Unknown to us, at lunchtime Major Abiriga had briefed the officers about this interview. At the same time an assortment of weapons was quickly assembled to welcome us.

The civilian idea of an interview is that of sitting down facing each other across a table, the interviewer(s) asking questions that are answered by the interviewee. That afternoon we found out how wrong we were when it came to military interviews. The officers had already judged and convicted some of us in absentia. On arrival at the mess, they were relaxing in all sorts of postures. Out of fear, we attempted to greet them 'Habari yenyu Wakubwa?' It was as if we had disturbed all the bees in their hive at 1.00 pm on a hot day. Everyone of the officers was talking and questioning us at the same time. Others were asking after tribe, religion, etc. Others were raining insults. It was a real Tower of Babel affair, only the language was common, Kiswahili. Because you cannot answer twenty or so questions at the same time, we kept quiet. After this babbling affair died down, Kwizera, the good boy, was told to speak. Some two or so minutes later, he was shut down. That was all the officers needed. They had heard enough. Within that brief moment Kwizera and Kamugisha were acquitted by this Kangaroo Court.

The remaining three of us were all from the north, moreover two of us were from West Nile. The Government belonged to West Nilers. Who could tolerate that sort of rebel activity? The officers descended on us with their assortment of weapons; '*Kibokos*' wooden canes, belts, batons, gun butts shouting obscenities and insults. We were very terribly tortured and I passed out momentarily.

I do not know for how long I was unconscious but when I came to my senses, all the officers were gone. Only the C/O and some few guards outside the mess remained. The C/O then gave orders to return us to the quarter guard and to beat us no more. Kwizera and Kamugisha were also not there so we assumed they were released. At the quarter guard we were put in single cells. Around sunset, a man was dragged nearly half dead into the empty cell next to mine. Immediately the soldiers (five of them) set to work on the man. In a very faint voice, the man pleaded in vain to spare his life but this only served to heighten the brutality with which the man was tortured.

As darkness arrived, the man was a corpse. The soldiers were laughing when the man breathed his last. The body was dragged out. We later learnt the man had cut a sergeant's leg with an axe during a drinking brawl at Katama village. This was how much life meant to Amin's regime. We must have been lucky to escape death at the Officer's Mess.

We spent another three restless nights at the quarter guard. We did not know whether we were about to be released because soldiers become friendly to us and even offered us food. However, our hopes were dashed when General Mustapha Adrisi came to close the signals course. A bird must have sung into the General's ears and the General did not like what he heard. He said he wanted to see us at Republic House, then Army Headquarters in Kampala. So on 23rd October 1976, we left for Kampala at 5.00 am in the Company of C/O Abiriga, flanked by four soldiers all armed with G3's.

We arrived at Republic House around 8.30 am. The place was buzzing with activity. Vehicles were moving in and out fairly fast. Soldiers' movements seemed coordinated.

Major Abiriga alighted from our vehicle and went straight into Republic House to the office of Colonel Isaac Malyamungu (then Chief of Training Operations) but the Colonel was not in. Another serious matter had been reported before our arrival and in a rage, the Colonel had gone to attend to the matter personally. Given his frequent outburst of temper at the time, God knows what our fate would have been had the Colonel been in. Most likely we would never have reached Makindye barracks. After about three hours, Major Abiriga came out and we were driven to Makindye Military Barracks.

The three hours or so when Major Abiriga was in Republic House may have been a blessing to us. Lt. Col. Gore, then of Suicide Mechanised Regiment, Masaka came out of Republic House and immediately recognised me in our Land Rover (we had met earlier sometime at his friend's house, a Major in Jinja who also was a friend of mine). He made very acid remarks to us which prompted one of our guards to ask exactly what our crime was. When we told him, he advised us to change our statement if ever we would be asked to make any. In that way we now became state witnesses rather than criminals.

Makindye Military Police was under the command of Col. Gabriel with Lt. Col. Habib as his 2nd in charge. Being a Muslim, Lt. Col. Habib had the upper hand in the affairs in the organisation while Col. Gabriel, a Christian, was just a figurehead. Within the camp there was another section, the SIB (Special Investigations Branch) headed by Major Ratib Mududu. Most of the times Major Mududu was not in the station so his second in charge, Sergeant Mohammed, a burly man with rusty hair and a Langi by tribe, conducted most of SIB business. The SIB men were plain clothed and the investigative arm of the organisation.

We arrived at Makindye around 1.30 pm. Having passed through four different gates, we found ourselves in Sgt. Mohammed's office. There were already other criminals in. The office itself was very somber and had a table with only two chairs. Most of the room was taken up by torture weapons and alleged exhibits. No English was allowed since Sgt. Mohammed did not speak English. All interrogations were conducted in Kiswahili, accompanied most times with beatings. Sgt. Mohammed could not build enough anger in our case because nobody accused us. He had no prior notice and we had no file accompanying us. He did not know where to start and we had to accuse ourselves. The advice our guard gave at Republic House was really working. All the same he gave us papers and we wrote our statements in English. Whether they were read and referred to I cannot tell. What was certain was that up to our release nobody called any of us to discuss the statements.

A lot of cases with the SIB were very minor indeed but would be blown up to the extent where you could lose your life if the case was not properly handled. Most of them were also police cases but the SIB got there first. It was not uncommon that many detainees did not have charge sheets or that the files were missing. You had to part with money if you needed freedom. One man we found there and left there had no near relatives and so could not afford the money. His offence was dancing with a Captain's girlfriend in a night club. Another man, a Langi, had murdered a tribesman over a woman at Namuwongo. The SIB arrested him instead of the police. I do not know how much he paid but the man was simply freed. Such were the goingson in Makindye, getting rich at the expense of untold suffering, deliberately imposed on the unfortunate civilian population.

For our crime – treason – we were dumped in that famous block C2. In C2, you are a condemned person and at the mercy of anyone who cared to take you there. You are locked up 24 hours a day. You do not do any 'fatigue' work and you only see the sun when receiving lunch and supper. Diarrhoea was very rampant (fortunately we had no case of cholera). The worst of C2 was that you could be made to disappear at any time. To give one example, the Christian priest used to preach to us on Tuesdays. One Tuesday in the month of November, the priest appeared in the form of Lt. Col. Juma Okaa (Butabika). He made a vain attempt at preaching Jesus to us. We all knew what his visit meant, locating a potential victim. That night, a Malian businessman was picked and heard of no more. Mali had (and I still think has) no envoy in Uganda, so who cared. Moreover he was rivalling Amin and company in the ivory trade. The ivory trade at the time was exclusively the monopoly of Amin, Lt. Col. Habib and one other civilian (name withheld for security reasons).

On another night, all eight men in a cell were carried away just because one wrong man happened to be in that room. So death was always living next to you and could strike at any time.

Major Mududu used to see detainees on Fridays. For six weeks, including Christmas week, he was attending to one of his wives who was being treated by a witch doctor in Toro. The woman was getting worse and Mududu was getting restless. When eventually he came to see us he was in a high temper. He took all of us out of our cells and ordered us to dance our traditional dances. We then went through boxing, then wrestling. Weak as we were, many people got injured, some bleeding badly. To top his anger the man ordered all of us to lash each other twelve strikes with 'kiboko' (leather thong).

The following weeks were full of anxiety. Did Mududu's wife die? Where was he (he did not appear again up to our release)? What was our fate now? We lost all hope.

For those of us who were in detention we did not know when and why trouble started between the late Archbishop Luwum and Amin. On February 17, 1977 the barracks were unusually empty. We later learnt that all officers and other soldiers who mattered had been summoned to the International Conference Center for urgent government business. The barracks was temporarily left in the command of a corporal. Nobody divulged any further information. One could easily sense the tension in the barracks. The place was just too quiet for one not to get the impression that something was amiss. Our inner cells were opened in the morning that day so we sat in the corridor talking in low voices, pondering what had happened. We were not even served any food that day.

Around 6.00 pm, as we sat around the iron gate, a Land Rover drove at a great speed into the courtyard. Immediately after it stopped two men who had been pinned to the floor of the Land Rover were pulled up and shot. The first man, tall and black, dressed in a proper suit, received one bullet in the head and two in the chest. The second man, shorter and in a Kaunda suit received one bullet each in the head and chest. Both bodies tumbled down. A third body was pulled down already dead.

The dress he had resembled that worn by Christian priests. Here was a red belt around the body's waist. As soon as the bodies were thrown onto the ground, the Land Rover turned and drove off.

At this point, one of the soldiers came to us, ordered us all into our cells and locked us up. We were therefore unable to see how the dead bodies were removed. In our cells we now knew something was terribly wrong but so terrified were we that nobody dared to speak. The next day we learnt the Archbishop was dead.

The silence was almost total. Around 8.30 pm, the silence was broken. Guns opened and a barrage of bullets hit the barracks. Even our C2 was not spared. The shooting lasted around 30 minutes. We also heard one soldier demanding keys to C2 to finish us. The in-charge 'prisoners', then one Captain Onzima, refused to hand over the keys saying the detainees were innocent of what was happening then. He was threatened and as he tried to run away he was shot in the leg. All the same he managed to escape. In that one truly heroic act of defiance, Captain Onzima saved us all.

For those who remember, the radio announcement on 18th February 1977 blamed rebels from Tanzania for the attack at Makindye barracks. The truth is that Amin had been purging soldiers of the Acholi and Lango origin. Two nights before, Mubende and Bombo barracks had been purged. The night of 17th February was for Makindye. On that day, 22 soldiers were rounded up and locked pending death.

The 22 hatched a plan to conceal one man in the ceiling so that when the guard came to open the door, the man in the ceiling would jump down on him, disarm him and then they would try to shoot their way out. When the time came, the man in the ceiling instead of disarming the guard, jumped down and tried to sneak away. The 'condemned' men still managed to disarm the guard and tried to shoot their way out. They did not know that other soldiers were behind and positioned elsewhere. This is when all hell broke loose. None of the 22 ever lived to tell the story.

The days up to our release were uneventful. There were theories advanced that it was the same General Mustapha who pressured SIB to release us. This could have been so since the General and my cousin brother married from the same family. Secondly the SIB had taken enough money from us and since they claimed our files were with the SIB, perhaps it was now useless to detain us further. The SIB even claimed that they had been to Kinyara twice to investigate and found us innocent. Whichever version is correct I will never know. We were only told the country needed engineers and accountants like us to produce sugar and we were let out of the gates of Makindye Military barracks at 10.30 am. on 22nd February 1977.

9
Cookie Night

T. L. Kisembo Bahemuka

It was a day like any other in 1982 at Lungujja, a Kampala suburb. Those were days of *Panda Gari* when Ugandans lived like hunted animals. For one would not know when one would be picked for a guerrilla and sent for ultimate slaughter.

I recall the day vividly but the date eludes my memory. I had just got disappointed by the refusal to be issued a Ugandan passport just because I had been identified as a member of the Democratic Party. A passport is a right to every citizen. I had been admitted to Hartford University in Connecticut in USA.

One engineer, Lule Lwa Ntanda, — I have since lost connection with him — but I hope he reads this, had tried to process the passport for me through the 'normal' *Magendo* process. He had also tried to get me sponsorship through F. Nelson Jr., who actually signed my admission form and with whom he had worked as associate Professor at one University in New York.

I brooded over the failure to obtain a passport and therefore an avenue to further education. I lost my appetite and had no supper that night. We were renting part of a house in Lungujja belonging to one lady I knew only as Norah. We were five cousins; Abdallah Bukenya, Jamada Kaluuma, Ahmed Namuyimba, Denis Kugonza and myself. Bukenya has since died but the rest of us are still alive in various parts of the country.

We had initiated a cookies industry called Super Kamba. Those football fans who frequented Nakivubo War Memorial Stadium will remember the cookies which were made in the shape of a rope and which would went for 10/= and 20/= a piece. The Super Kamba business was the cause of the incident I am about to narrate which I **will never** forget. We had made more small ka-money which caused the youth, our agemates, to envy us and led to UNLA soldiers raiding our home.

It was during the Muslim month of Ramadhan and Abdallah, Jamada and Ahmed were fasting. We had had a hard and difficult day. After sales we had not counted the proceeds of that day. We had just thrown the money under an occasional table in a corner on which we kept our Philips automatic changer record player with about 200 records.

Remember those were the days of record players, the Philips type being the 'in thing' at that time.

At the time of Daku (the meal Muslims eat after midnight in order to fortify themselves against the vagaries of hunger during the day), we were packing Super Kamba into boxes for the next sale and sorting the money from previous sale.

Our facility was not self-contained and our toilets were outside. I was shot and was going out for a short call when it happened.

I opened the door and took one step outside. There was bright moon which enabled me to see what was out there. What I saw nearly made me collapse where I was standing. I was stunned. The compound was alive with men in battle camouflage and armed with rifles, the popular AK47. The shock was but a second long. I uttered a cry and jumped back in the house. I closed the door but someone or some people pushed from outside. I kicked off my slippers and pushed the carpet away from the door. This was to enable my feet to get a better grip on the floor.

In my civilian mind I did not know that a bullet could pass through the wood panelling of the door. I managed to push the door shut and put in the two bolts but could not turn the key in the mortise lock. The kicking had started and the flimsy bolts flew across the room. I put my shoulder against the door and tried to push it shut so that I could turn the key in the mortise lock but at that time the kicking from outside was so intense that hinges broke and the door split into two.

Everybody else had run into Bukenya's bedroom and were hiding under beds. There were calls from the 'Commander' of the contingent who was telling his soldiers not to shoot. The calls were in both Luo and Swahili. I have never known what made me do a fool hardy thing like that. Anyway I switched off the overhead light and joined the rest in the bedroom. There was an old aunt to Bukenya who had come for a courtesy call and had spent the night with us. She soiled her clothes and fainted.

The door crashed down but part of it remained attached to the jamb on the semi-attached hinge. The soldiers entered the house and one of them located the switch and turned it on. They were ordered not to touch anything.

The 'Commander' then ordered us to come out one by one with our hands in the air. I was going to move out first but Bukenya held me back, because it was his house he should die first if it had to be. He said I had already done enough.

When he entered the sitting room, his name was called. The surprise was that the name used was his childhood name which was popular when we were in primary school in Lira. The conversation was in Lango. We were told to come out separately. When I came out I involuntarily shaded my eyes from the harsh light. Remember I was coming from a dark room. I had forgotten the hands-up order. Ogwal, the 'Commander', called my name and the names of the others as they came out. Only Jamada and Bukenya's wife were not known to him. This surprised his soldiers who were holding their rifles at hip level, a position I have since learnt is called high port.

The 'Commander', Ogwal, who was a sergeant at the time then explained to his fellow soldiers that we had gone to Lira P7 School with him.

Ogwal told his boys to go out and marshal the soldiers. That is when he told us that the whole house had been surrounded by a platoon of soldiers. He explained to us that information had reached them from an informer in Lungujja that the occupants of our premises were rebels (NRA) collaborators and that the money we made from Super Kamba was remitted to the bush and that was why we lived in simple lifestyle. The only luxurious item in the house was actually the record player and the pile of records. I also had an impressive collection of novels in the same corner, especially fiction works.

He inquired who had been struggling at the door and I said it was me. He then explained to me how bullets can pass through wooden doors with no resistance. I was warned never to defy a soldier's order as it could easily lead to my death.

Some had picked the record player and gone with it in the heat of the moment. I was told to go and open the gate and I asked them how they entered the compound. Some did not like it and pointed out that since I was the brave one I should go and open the gate. That is when Ogwal saw the player and ordered it returned. The offending soldier threw the player down and the top separated from the engine.

Well, alas. I opened the gate and behold there were more soldiers outside on jeeps. I thought I would be shot then. I wasn't and that is why I am writing these lines. I did not close the gate nor pick the record player. However, soon we moved to another area but still in Lungujja.

10
Panda Gari Experience

Yosam Baguma

The *Panda Gari* era was a period in the early 1980s characterised by massive random arresting of people and confining them into open grounds especially stadium, and screening them to identify rebels at the time. The period is commonly known as Obote II regime. Prior to these massive arrests, I had narrowly survived being arrested together with late Besigensi, late Kibandama, late Dr. Babugumira, etc. in Kabale. The UPC that had won the controversial 1980 elections was afraid of the strong personalities in the opposition parties whom it suspected likely to join the armed rebellion because the bush war had been declared. Although I had not contested my position in the elections, I had been a publicity secretary in the UPM Kabale interim executive. One night while asleep, I sensed trouble somehow. Then I decided to wake up very early to go to Kampala. I boarded a lorry which was loading bales of second-hand clothes destined for Jinja.

On reaching Butobere junction, soldiers had put up a serious road block. Three people and I had been placed in a space between the bales and the board of the lorry just behind the driver. No sooner had the driver left his seat after stopping, than I heard a whip slap burst into the ear of the driver. He started stammering funny words and pulled out money which had been budgeted for the road block. As the soldiers received the money, not even counting it, they shouted '*Onabeba nini? Kwenda!!*' (What are you carrying? Go!!)

The rest of the journey to Mukono was undisturbed. I disembarked the lorry and boarded other taxis back to Kampala. I still owned my flat in Kampala at Nkrumah Road. I had just arrived in the house at 3.30 pm when I heard a knock on the door. I opened the door only to find my brother-in-law, Benon Bwembale. After greeting each other, he handed to me a chit from my wife narrating what she had gone through. I left in the lorry that morning. After reading it, I realised it had been my subconscious which saved me. Otherwise I should have been a victim of the arrest that morning. The chit warned me to take care of my security since photos in the album where some people including late Besingensi appeared were moved and placed in their file. They also took other documents including my certificates. My wife had been quizzed and threatened with a whip in case she told them a lie, because when they came at 6.00 am, I had left at 5.00am that morning.

From that moment, I was alert for twenty-four hours. But I knew it would be in known public places where they would trap me. So I decided to avoid them. I decided to suspend drinking alcohol. I went to withdraw all the money on my account. I paid for express installation of a post office box and telephone in my house. Since I had not returned to my civil service job since 1979, I decided not to appear in that office at all. Fortunately my contacts were sufficient to guarantee me business for survival. I started managing my clearing agency on a full-time basis and I opened branches in different towns like Kampala, Malaba and Entebbe, which was vital for my concealment. We also had a publication business. What remained as a standing issue was the security file with my photos. I had a relative in the CID office. When I sent him a message that I wanted to see him, he took it upon himself to cross check my security record in relevant offices. He discovered that those arrested were paying ransom for their release. Those not yet arrested could pay some money and buy off their file and burn the contents for the safety of the security official in case of reconfiscation of the same documents. When my file was on transit to Kampala from Kabale, he arrived in a hurry to collect 30,000/= for that purpose. I produced the money which he took and returned with the file within ten minutes. He had left the officer in a waiting vehicle at a distance from my flat. After perusing through, he directed me to destroy the file in his presence, which I did without hesitation. I felt a sense of relief in my mind at least for some time. Up to 1984, I was transacting my business normally but for security purposes I would never travel to Kabale from Kampala in taxis or buses. I used to fly to Kakyeka airstrip in Mbarara from Entebbe, then proceeded to Kabale from there.

My clearing company was doing very well. At one time, we struck a business deal to clear street lights for all towns in Uganda. We won a contract to clear all UEB cargo at Entebbe Airport. I could bulldoze my consignment from the Airport by dishing money as Managing Director. Unfortunately some people, envious about our success, maliciously reported that we were not paying taxes and our license was suspended pending investigations. Then I had a rough time chasing officials concerned up to the Minister of State for Finance, by then Hon. Kamuntu, who after interviewing me and finding no case with my company ordered the Commissioner of Customs to lift the ban on our license. For a week any of the directors would frequent the office of the commissioner to check on the license because I had done the rest of the most important works. Mind you it was a risk for me to frequent big offices like that of Finance whose Finance Minister was none other than the President himself.

Unfortunately and surprisingly, when I rang one of the shareholders to go and the collect the license from the secretary, he claimed that all the effort was his, and directors believed him. So when the company made a party to celebrate, all speeches were praising him for having met the Minister, interviewed successfully and finally he had brought the license! No mention was made of me, directors didn't want my name mentioned as their associate for political reasons. They were just enjoying my services. I therefore abandoned the company without raising any dust, also for political reasons.

By 1984, the government intelligence agents had intensified their activities and had penetrated all public places. Fortunately, I had my own information network including information at the front line itself.

As time went by my absence from the clearing business was felt, especially by security people at the Entebbe Airport. Yet I could be sighted around Kampala at times, so they started monitoring my movements. One day, which was the eve of the Democratic Party International Convention in Kampala, I was passing through the present Owino Market when I met one lieutenant. He greeted me enthusiastically and asked me where I had been. I replied I was around. He again wanted to know where all the money I had went. 'I am still doing business but not as before because seasons change', I said. Then I noticed he had some escorts following him from behind. That place was very busy. As he turned to signal his escorts to arrest me, people interrupted him as they moved from all directions. By mere instinct, I jumped over a chain link fence which was covered by thick crawling plants and landed in the compound of Nakivubo Settlement Primary School, fortunately unnoticed by him! Those plants had made such a thick covering all round the chainlink that it was difficult to see through unless he had seen me jump over. I turned to confirm they had not noticed my direction. I peeped through the fence and saw him turning around checking every passer by. There was commotion, then they gave up. I passed through the school compound to the present container village and joined Nakivubo Mews on my way home.

The following day was the DP International Convention in Kampala. More than 50 countries were represented on the convention at City Square. As I came from Nakasero and the colleague I had gone to see was escorting me, we decided to sit down for a cold soda in Wimpy (present Curry Pot), while finalising our discussion. The chair I sat on was facing a television set which seemed out of order. After one sip of the soda I fixed my eyes at the seemingly dead TV set. Then suddenly a flash light of camera struck my eyes like lightening from inside the TV screen. I realised the intelligence had acquired more sophisticated technology and now they are able to gather photos of suspicious people whenever they need them.

Therefore I was no longer safe in Kampala. So like lightening also I sneaked out of the Wimpy, crossed the Kampala road, across Wilson Road, passed by DP office near Munno publications, passed behind the present shopping mall and crossed to the Co-operative Bank from where I hired a taxi to my house.

At night I considered all options for a way forward and decided to rejoin the civil service but requested for a transfer from Kampala. I processed my reinstatement and posting letter in one day. I was posted to Nshara Government Ranch at 31 miles from Mbarara on Masaka road. This is where I stayed 'in hiding' till the Obote II and Lutwa regimes were overthrown.

11
Those Days in Luwero

Henry Mutibwa

I found her at Kanyanda, a tiny junction just a few kilometers before Semuto town in Luwero District. There was a small crowd around her and at first I could not figure out what was at the center of the group. Thinking it was another victim of mob justice, I hesitated in my approach for fear of seeing human blood. For it was a common phenomenon in those days to dispense instant 'justice' to whoever surfaced and was known to have taken part in the sacrilegious dilapidation of the economic, social and cultural order of hundreds of square kilometers comprising the Luwero triangle; and the immensely brutal annihilation of about 800,000 lives, an act was executed with a heavy tinge of hatred.

My encounter with this pitiful woman was in May 1986, about four months after the NRA had liberated a large portion of the country. The two days I had spent with a visiting relative in Luwero, what was once her home, had shown me a series of statistics on misery. What had once been a bungalow had either been crushed flat by a huge tree three or four years previously, or had been stripped of its roofing and the half broken walls were fencing in an ecosystem comprising of an assortment of trees and shrubs as well as small fauna like squirrels and lizards. It was a common sight to find a family sandwiched in an elongated pyramid-shaped structure made out of the remnants of rotting iron sheets. Those whose iron sheets had disappeared had to use woven frames filled with grass. The once beautiful countryside was no more.

The surviving population, while talking of the whole episode as if it was a joke, hardly betrayed any self-pity and exhibited a lot of determination for the future. It is you the visitor who could easily get surprised on seeing half-naked adults moving with sticks as if it was an essential part of the tattered attire. I had enquired about these sticks and got various explanations. Some said a stick was a companion while making solitary run from the foraging army that showered the countryside with artillery fire for five years. One villager termed such running as 'hide and seek with no laughter at the end.' Others said a stick was a useful tool in flattening the undergrowth before lying down for a brief rest, or a friendly tool to push thorny branches out of the way during a more peaceful trek. Still others used it for protection against dangers like snakes, but no one confessed having carried it in self defence in case of an accidental encounter with a marauding soldier. A few did not exactly know why they carried a stick. It was just a style.

Seeing no sign of violence on the faces of bystanders, I gained courage when my companion suggested that we go closer, only to be confronted by a pitifully scraggy little woman seated by her equally dilapidated toddler whose appearance left you wondering how it was possible that he was still alive.

The despicable state of Efulansi (that was her name) and her child was unmatched by the misery of the countryside and the general populace. She had a particular way of staring ahead while seemingly looking at nothing in particular. She had not spoken since the time we had arrived and I thought she was dumb or mentally unbalanced. I do not recall her clothing for I was more concerned about her silent agony and the mournful look on her long, pale face. Moreover, there was this child who seemed to suffer from a mixture of acute measles, malnutrition an anaemia. The sunken half-closed eyes and the sore frail body of this child presented a picture of two-year moribund. My companion was a very talkative woman well known for her knack in expressing grief, especially at funerals. She did not therefore hesitate to engage the sullen woman and shower her with a sample of her verbal consolatory package. To the astonishment of everyone around, the only response from the poor woman was a mere 'hmm' each time my companion paused. What changed the course of events was the question as to whether she had tried to seek treatment for the child. It was at this juncture that Efulansi lifted her eyes, looked at her interviewer and said coolly, *'Mukazi wattu, mala gandeka'* loosely meanly 'Please dear lady, spare me the trouble' and then the following story unfolded.

It was in April 1983, at the peak of the worst moments of manhunt in Semuto where Efulansi, her husband, and six children were surviving in the wilderness. The people in this part of Uganda had been running around since 1981, trying not to be caught in the crossfire between the then Government troops and the then NRA guerrillas. Needless to say, however, that the innocent civilians feared the Government soldiers most for they unleashed untold suffering onto them, in form of vengeance for the activities of the rebels operating amongst them.

Efulansi recounted that the two days preceding her fate had been relatively calm and the various families had cautiously returned to their homes for stock taking. All of a sudden, the skies were torn by deafening bangs and the surrounding hills billowed smoke while the clatter of machine gunfire confirmed the fate of the entrapped villagers. They ran towards a huge valley where they used to hide, with the courageous ones chasing their dear cattle in the same direction in the hope of saving them. These cows did their share of trampling to death several children and maiming a few adults but there was no time then to know who had been downed. The 'enemy' had carefully planned the assault for they waited until all the people had entered the deep valley then they showered the tree tops with rockets that tore the branches which eventually fell onto the 'escapees'. The terrified cries and wailing only provoked prolonged laughter from the assailants. The laughter could be heard echoing on the hillsides while the attackers resumed their game with renewed relish.

Completely outwitted, the peasants succumbed to the military might of the 'invaders' and they were rounded up and led to one of the big homes in the area. The captured numbered about forty, for they comprised of people from near and far, all engaged in the game of saving dear life. It did not matter where you came from. As long as you came across some strangers in a somewhat similar predicament, you were welcome to run with them. On arrival at the compound, they were separated into two groups; men and boys on one side, the women and babies on the other. The groups were ridiculed with cruel jokes but with such well-masked bitterness that the present day survivors thought everybody was going to be left to go.

The women were made to sit (like they do at a village meeting), facing the line of their husbands and sons, then the agenda was **tackled**. A briefing preceded the event and it was made clear that any breach of the contract would lead to very harsh reprisals. It was a tough contract but everyone had to sign his part. The rules were simple and straightforward. The man in front is shot, then those two next to him lift him and transfer his writhing body to a distance. They are then ordered to stretch the body out, face down and arms stretched infront.

Quickly, they have to return to their original positions and wait for their turn. The 'bullet feast' continued, following the order of the line until every member of the line was in lying position beside the one he had helped to lift.

By the end of phase one, no female captive was capable of gazing at the grisly sight. All had hidden their faces in the grass that was once the turf of a beautiful compound. Phase two therefore involved kicking them into sitting position and they were shown their gallant husbands and sons at the front-line (to quote the words of one of the captors). These men had once again carried a cruel joke of choosing such a lying position, invoking a man taking cover and holding a gun. The women were dumbfounded and very few dared or cared to cry. The assailants were not yet done, for they had all the time and peace around them.

The next item on the agenda consisted of checking the babies on the mother's laps to ensure whether they were male or female. If a woman was lucky enough to be carrying a girl child, they would throw it back to her saying she would become their wife once she grew up. If another happened to be carrying a baby boy, they would grab him and carry out an urgent 'assignment.' The turning point in Efulansi's life came when they discovered she had a baby boy. Had her situation been slightly different, the horror of what followed would probably have been attenuated. It was not that she was necessarily less fortunate than her colleagues, but I hope the reader will agree that the fever gripping her brain cells was several degrees higher.

In the row of the dead males, there were six of her sons plus her husband, and here they were demanding for the neck of her last next-of-kin. Efulansi went wild, calling the names and demanding that they kill her first before finishing off her little one. Her resistance did not help for long; two boot kicks in the abdomen were enough to make her let go. The more she wailed the more infuriated the aggressor become and Efulansi thinks this is what made him do what he did.

After ripping off the neck of her dear child with a sharp knife from his belt, the aggressor proceeded to whip the mother with the headless body while holding its legs. Each swing was followed by a dull thud against Efulansi's head, back and chest until the spurting blood from the baby soaked her body and blocked her view. She lost consciousness, though she could not tell for how long.

On regaining consciousness, a grubby man (one of the aggressors) introduced himself to her as her future husband. She was at a loss. She knew she had brushed shoulders with death but could not even recall at that very moment that her whole family was 'lying in state.' The memory of it all flowed back as she was being led away to a life of misery that lasted five weeks inside a camp of undisciplined, stinking, uniformed riffraffs who played with bullets as you would play with stones.

The end result was this sick child who never saw his father. Efulansi managed to escape one evening while she went with other women to collect water unescorted. We did not hear the rest of the story for everybody was pleading with her to stop, fearing she might break down. Her soft and monotonous voice still rings in my ears as she explained in conclusion that this is why nobody should ask her about treatment of this child whose father participated in decimating her entire legitimate family before planting his seed. She could not even care about the future of this child for she did not even share anything in common with the father who was long gone. Where? She did not bother herself with the question.

12
Forced to Rape
Godfrey Olukya

I thought myself very unfortunate when after qualifying as a secondary school teacher I was posted to Ndejje S. S. S. That was in 1985 during Obote II regime when the war between the then government soldiers and rebels was at its peak.

Ndejje Secondary School was in an area which was termed as a danger zone. The danger zone was the area in which the war was taking place and was under a situation similar to that of a state of emergency or even worse.

I tried to dodge going to the school I was posted to and tried to ask the posting officer, then Noah Ssemugoma, to post me to another school but he refused. After trying him several times in vain, I decided to go to Ndejje S.S.S. On reporting at the school, I realised that the school was intact but all the structures in the neighborhood had been destroyed. There were no people in the surrounding villages, all of them had been herded into a camp not very far from the school.

It was in that camp that I witnessed inhumanity that I had never experienced ever before in my life and do not wish to witness again.

Within the school were very co-operative and interesting teachers who comforted me and convinced me to stay. One of them was the late Jimmy Combe (later joined the *New Vision* newspaper where he had a column in the *Sunday Vision*), with whom I clicked and I started enjoying my stay in Ndejje.

Due to the environment we took to heavy drinking. We used to drink in a joint within the school run by the school chief askari and Combe and I were once drinking in that place when we were joined by one of the soldiers who was in charge of the detach that guarded the camp in which over three thousand villagers had been assembled. We drank together till late in the night. He requested that we visit him in the camp the following day.

The following day, Combe and I walked into the camp. It consisted of numerous huts made of elephant grass. The huts were squeezed near to each other and each family was entitled to only one.

The villagers were all emaciated and dressed in rags. The young ones were all suffering from kwashiorkor and beriberi. A mere look at them could make one shed tears; protruding bellies, yellow hair, mucus-filled faces and red eyes.

The officer we had gone to visit was not around but his junior welcomed us, gave us benches and immediately brought out a small jerrycan full of locally distilled liquor, popularly known as *enguli*. As we drank and chatted, one of the soldiers saw a lame man walking to his hut, *'Hee, Musizi kujja hapo'*, he called the lame man.

The lame man came. The soldier then told us that when he was in the city a few days back, he happened to watch a video featuring Michael Jackson dancing.

Those were the days when Michael Jackson was at the peak of the music world and he had introduced the break dance. In that dance some people danced as if they were lame by feigning lameness.

So the soldier told the lame man to start dancing. At first the man refused but after several slaps and kicks he started dancing while trying to balance on the good leg. As he did so, the lame leg swung in the air.

The soldiers clapped their hands as they urged him to dance on. He danced on and on till he got tired and fell down. Although the soldiers kicked him trying to make him stand up and continue to dance, Musizi was so exhausted that he could not get up. One of the soldiers picked a big stick and administered one hundred strokes on Musizi. He collapsed, unconscious.

The four soldiers, who were by that time drunk, requested that Combe and I carry Musizi to his hut. They told us that he had a beautiful woman and since her husband had failed to entertain us to our satisfaction, his wife would cover up. I held the legs of Musizi and Combe held the trunk and we carried him to his hut. The four soldiers followed us with their guns and showed us the hut.

We carried him inside. Seated in the hut was his wife and four children. The lady seemed to be around twenty-five years old. The oldest, a girl who was about twelve years old, was followed by one of nine, another of five and the last of three years.

Immediately the wife saw her husband in a coma and started crying. But the soldiers ordered her to stop crying. She stopped. They then told her that they had just rescued her husband from the rebels and they wanted to be paid in kind. She stood up. One of the soldiers held her by the shoulders while another one kicked both of her legs and she fell down on her back. She had no sooner fallen down than one of the soldiers fell on her with one hand pulling up her dress and the other unzipping his trousers. The soldier inserted his manroot into her as she groaned in pain. The children were watching in disbelief as the soldiers mounted their mother.

The other soldiers ordered us to remain with them till the mission was over lest we went and reported them to their boss and they would be caught red-handed. They put us at gun-point.

After the first soldier was through with the woman another one took over. The woman screamed and screamed as the second soldier who seemed to be well-endowed underneath wriggled his back and buttocks.

One of the soldiers who had not had a chance yet became impatient. One could see his rod protruding through his trousers. He complained that his colleague was over-delaying on the woman and that he was bursting with lust *'Wewe bwana fannya haraka mimi piya nifannyeko nnsikiya vibaya bwana'*, he said. (You sir, do it fast so that I too have a chance. I am badly off). But the second man would not come off the woman. The soldier became impatient and grabbed the twelve-year-old daughter of Musizi, threw her down, parted her legs and tried to push his rod into her.

But the organ was too big and could not enter. It seemed an idea struck his mind. He checked his pocket and brought out a razor blade. I could not believe my eyes when I saw him cutting the sides of the girl's private parts, trying to extend them so that they could accommodate his big 'thing'.

He succeeded. In spite of the girl's bleeding profusely he went ahead with his mission. It was appalling to look at such a scene, a mother being raped side by side with her daughter. Soon the last soldier also got his chance. He ascended on the tired woman and also raped her. When they had all finished with their adventure they told us that in order to balance the equation we also had to sleep with the woman and her daughter.

We tried to refuse to do so but they told us that they could easily kill us and hide our bodies if we did not comply. It seemed they wanted us to sleep with the woman and her daughter so that we would not discuss it with other people or report them anywhere because we had also participated, though unwillingly.

When I realised that my life was in danger, I accepted and involuntarily slept with the woman. But was it worth it anyway?

Combe, seeing the bleeding private part of the girl, refused to sleep with her. Being funny as he was he urged me to be fast that he also get his share. (He later told me that he said that simply to please the soldiers but, like me, he was not at all interested).

The soldiers later escorted us to the gate of the camp and as we separated they warned us never to talk about what had transpired. From that day onwards (till the day I left Ndejje) I vowed never to associate with the brutal soldiers.

13
Escaped Escorting a Corpse

Roy Golooba Kalema

This story unfolds at a time characterised by institutional harassment of the civilian population by security personnel, days variously known as the *'Panda Gari'*, 'OILA' or the 'Computer' days! They were so named because of the methods employed by the regime to try to keep insurgency under control.

The regime in power at that time felt so harassed by the guerrilla activities of the various insurgent groups, particularly that of the National Resistance Army (NRA) led by Yoweri Museveni, that it put up road blocks anywhere, any time to 'flush' out guerrillas or their collaborators. It could then capture and interrogate people. Later broadcasts on radio and television would describe them as having confessed to being guerrillas. These people were known as 'computers' who were used to screen out purported guerrillas from the general public! So, the army captured people at road blocks, at the whims of the local commander in control at a given road block. Other occasions, dawn raids by the army on surrounding areas of Kampala, e.g. Ndeeba, Rubaga, Nsambya, Makindye and Namasuba were organised and the captured people, were thrown onto trailers and driven to Nsambya Railway grounds where the 'Computers' would then screen them, pin-pointing the guerrillas and collaborators in that order. If one was picked by the 'computer' it then meant that he would either be taken to Nile Mansion (Paulo Muwanga's domains) for a meeting with him or to Makindye military barracks for interrogation and thereafter killed or used as another serial 'screener'. So, Nsambya Railway ground came to be notoriously known as the *'Panda Gari'* grounds!

At that time, I used to work for a government department whose offices were situated within walking distance from my flat on Allen Road Nakivubo. It was therefore convenient for me to get there easily. I was in the habit of going back home for lunch followed by a thirty-minute siesta, while listening to personal announcements on our local Blue Channel Radio Uganda, before getting back to office, in time for work. So on that terrible day, I was to get the unforgettable experience of my life!

This episode unfolded during the lunch-time break on a normal working day in 1982. I had as usual left office for home early, so as to reach in time to enjoy my lunch and spare some time to rest. Everything appeared normal when suddenly at around 1.30 pm, after my lunch and while tuned to Radio Uganda, I heard a very loud and terrifying noise which appeared to be automatic gunfire, coming from the vicinity of Splending Lodge on Nakivubo Road. Then I peeped through the drawn curtains of my bedroom window overlooking Shauri-Yako Market for tell-tale signs of what was happening outside. In fact it was usual for us to judge the prevailing situation by just looking at the activities taking place there. If the situation was normal, everybody would be moving about, in a relaxed mood but if anything unusual was happening, people would panic and the gates of the market would be shut immediately.

What I saw sent my nerves on edge. The situation out there was chaos itself. It was as if fire had broken out in Shauri-Yako Market! People were crying, running in all directions. Everybody was panicking and confused and with no apparent place to hide. The gates of the market had been locked by the gate keeper to safe-guard whatever property was there from looters. People were frantically searching for dark spots to hide in, with no apparent sign of success! Others were trying to climb and jump over the market walls. It was just terrible! There were some die-hards who were not ready to leave their wares and of course these stayed put. Though later they also had to abandon the fort, as the situation deteriorated further. I left the window, and decided that it would not be prudent of me to start walking back to office, as I very well knew that out there I could easily end up as fodder for trigger-happy security operatives who I was sure were then on their way. An idea came to me to stay at the dining table that was near the main entrance and wait out there.

I was scared but I knew from experience that there was nothing to be done. The question of concealment was out, as there was no where to hide! Suddenly I heard banging at the front door entrance. I could not tell who they were at the time but what was unique was that, whoever was at the door, sounded scared. When I did not open up, they continued banging, shouting to be let in. They pleaded till they were tired and resorted to outright begging. I was confronted with a difficult decision on whether or not to let them in but after listening to the begging I decided to let them in as I knew they had nowhere else to turn. On opening the door, I was suddenly pushed by a heavy force of human flesh. People of all description, especially traders from Shauri-Yako barged in. Some carried bales of used clothes, others bags, some clutching at bundles of money, while others were empty handed, but wailing for the property they believed they had by then lost, back at the market.

I went and tried to calm down the refugees I had let in, telling them to keep quiet but no avail. Some were busy discussing what to do next, others were arguing, while others were asking me for another way out of the flat in case. Others wanted to know where they could hide their money, and some, where they could hide themselves. It was total confusion.

Since the start of all this confusion I was yet to find out what exactly was happening out there. I enquired from one person but all he could say was *'owange eby'ogira obileka Katonda yamanyi'* meaning my friend, meanwhile forget all that, it is God who knows! Then one lady came to me and told me that according to what she had heard, the 'Muwanga boys' had been shot dead on Nakivubo Road by guerrillas of Museveni! She further added that at the time of deserting her stall in the market, various units of state operatives were combing the area and that a lot of looting of all types of property by them was in progress. Having got that information I became eager to follow what was going on outside. So back to the bedroom window I returned. I peeped through the curtains and what I saw chilled me. Platoons and platoons of soldiers were pouring into Nakivubo area from Lubiri via Kisenyi and all appeared to be battle ready. I went back to the sitting and dining rooms to inform the people of the new developments. Then gunshots rang out from all directions. I decided to seal the main entrance by bolting the door completely, erecting supports in case any extra force would be used from the outside.

As it was approaching 2.15pm., there was a big bang at the entrance and an authoritative voice bellowed in Swahili thus, *'funguwa mulango haraka, onasikia hi ni jeshi fungua!'*, translated to mean, open the door quickly, this is the army.

When I opened the door three Special Force personnel rushed in with bayonets at the ready, shouting *'kila mutu lala chini, kila mutu lala chini, munasikia?'*, meaning everybody lie down, everybody lie down, have you heard? So it was for dear life that everybody around went down on the bellies awaiting further instructions from the soldiers.

It was then that the leader of the trio asked, *'Mwenye nyumba hi yiko wapi? Mwenya nyumba hi yiko wapi? Munakata ku sema?'* Meaning 'where is the owner of this house, have you refused to answer' I got up and responded: *'mimi yiko hapa'.* He then asked me to assist him and I went to see what it was he wanted to be assisted about. Leading me into the sitting room he told everyone lying down to surrender whatever they had, after which he turned everything in the room upside down then called on his colleagues and they all started a systematic grabbing of watches, money and any other valuables first from me and the people. All this loot found its way into the roomy pockets of their army fatigues. It was this time, that the leader asked me to guide him to the other rooms in the house, all the while demanding where more money was and saying that those traders in the sitting room must have hidden big amounts of money in the house! I told him in turn that the money he had found on the persons was all they had come in with. As for me, I told him that I was only a struggling civil servant trying to make ends meet and had no money and that in fact that was the reason I had happened to be at home at the time, not being able to afford the expensive lunch sold in hotels or restaurants in town. I had come home to grab something for lunch. He then asked me, *'wewe onatoka wapi?'* Meaning 'where do you come from? I decided that in order not to antagonise him and propel him into tribal frenzy the only thing to do was to deceive him that I was from Tororo. Since I knew one of the languages of the area well, I could have easily passed for one from there. I was therefore greatly relieved when he answered back in Swahili. *'Ndugu pole, ata na wewe olikuja* Kampala *kwa taabu pole kamata sawa yako'*, this all meant: Brother sorry, you also came this way because of suffering, okay. Please get back your watch. I was elated. I realised then that had I disclosed my true tribe or origins, I would have been in deep trouble. The soldiers, having found a kind of solidarity in this perceived brotherhood with me, advised me to hide myself as so many others like him were in the process of coming up to the flats. I informed him that I had no choice as there was nowhere to hide, my flat being the topmost one and with no outlet anywhere. He told me that he was ready to volunteer to stand for me and tell incoming soldiers, that his group has finished checking and inspecting the house in which we were. I told him then that I was going to continue sitting at the dining table and wait for whatever was to follow. He told me to lock the door on his exit as he and his group had already taken whatever they could possibly fancy. They left the people who had taken refuge in the house in tears and great sorrow at the loss of all their valuables.

After locking up the front entrance, I went back to the dining table to ponder the trend of events. There was not much I could do apart from holding my head between my hands, recollecting the sequence of the unfolding drama! It was not to be long before I was startled by new banging and shouting emanating from the entrance. This meant that most likely, another group of soldiers was demanding entrance to the flat! There was more banging. I then told whoever it was to hold on as I unbolted the door. I went through the process of opening and eventually got the door wide open. In they rushed, this time numbering ten army persons! The leader was shouting in Swahili *'kwa nini nyini munafunga nyumba?' Nyinyi ndio adui Munawuwa askari'*, Meaning 'Why did you people lock the door? You are the enemies', 'you killed soldiers'.

I was now panicking, realising that after that kind of statement from the soldiers, anything was bound to happen. I got the guts and answered them that for me I was only a civil servant who had nothing to do with banditry! They pushed about, and the process of looting the entire house commenced. Everything from utensils, bed sheets and any other valuables they fancied were taken while I was looking on. I was asked for money once again and informed them that whatever had been available had already been taken by the earlier group that had invaded the flat. They were not satisfied so they checked the people in the sitting room until they were convinced that there really wasn't anything left to steal. They left.

Eventually, after getting courage, I looked through the wire mesh in the dining room area and seeing the people who had been forced to lie down on Allen Road by soldiers as if they were corpses, I decided that the best thing to do was to find any way out of the flat, before the worst happened to me. Moreover it appeared there was nothing much my presence in the house could do to help, as the whole house had been vandalised. I talked to the people and suggested that it was time for everybody to find his way out as being inside was no longer safe and so everybody started leaving. And I was the last one to go leaving the entrance slightly open. I rushed downstairs hoping to wait at the verandah. As some of my neighbours and I were seated down at the verandah, a group of security personnel who appeared to belong to NASA (National Security Agency) approached us and demanded to know what we were doing down there. We were accused of being trouble causers and indeed we were responsible for the death of security personnel that had occurred. Identity cards were demanded of us. We were ordered to vacate the place and cross Nakivubo Channel. We were expected to wait from Mackay Road! You can imagine the feelings we had, but all the same we obeyed and crossed over! Before crossing over, however, the soldiers with AK47s at the ready, appeared and threatened to shoot at us! Pandemonium broke out, and in the process some people broke their limbs! Eventually we managed to reach Mackay Road on the other side of Nakivubo Channel. At Mackay Road we were so traumatised by what we had gone through and by what we continued to see. Columns and columns of security personnel, namely NASA, Special Force, Military police and army, were busy looting from all the houses and shops around. Some of the looted property was already finding its way to the army houses on Mackay Road, houses that had formerly been occupied by police. By around 3.00pm, Nakivubo area was all confusion! It was then that I again enquired from one of the people I was seated with at the verandah what had actually happened to cause all the confusion. The man told me that Paulo Muwanga's operatives otherwise known as 'golf boys' because of the Volkswagen Golf vehicles they were known to drive, had been shot at and killed just opposite Splendid Lodge and that it was believed that it was the work of Museveni's network of "bandits", as they were called by the Obote II regime.

Meanwhile, as we were talking and allowing all this information to sink in, we saw army lorries arrive in the area to ferry the loot so far collected. All hope of recovering anything was lost and our only consolation was that so far nobody we knew had been killed. This belief was disproved later. As time went on, we became desperate and anxious about our situation. We did not know what to do but continued staring at our homes and could see curtains moving about and behind them people in army uniforms moving about. So we concluded it was not safe to go back home. It was approaching 5.00 pm and office workers were beginning to trickle back from their places of work. At our end then it appeared the situation had somewhat calmed. We talked things over with one of my neighbours and it was decided that we could try to get back to our houses and assess out the situation on the spot! Crossing the channel back was not that difficult. Once inside my flat I peeped through the wire meshing in the dining area and was not amused by what I saw! Soldiers were very much still around and were torturing people captured at Short Lane. This was not encouraging either. I was left with only one choice, to rush back to where I had come from lest I was cornered inside. Then as I was rushing downstairs, I met a Lieutenant of the army coming up, who then enquired of a colleague of his. I shot back that I did not know where he was and sped on downstairs, but on approaching the street I bumped into three mad, if not drunken, raff-tag soldiers with guns poised. They were shouting at the top of their voices in Swahili *'Mupoteye awo mutakua nyama ya porini'* Meaning 'disappear or else you shall be dead game meat'. I knew that they meant what they were saying and so tried to disappear from the scene as fast as my legs could carry me. This time it was difficult to cross the channel, as there were more people than previously and the threat of the soldiers was not to be taken lightly either. I decided that I was not going to follow this heavy human traffic to cross so I ran towards the Remand Prison end in order to cross from there. Then as I was mid-stream of the channel, I heard a shout from behind me. It was of a security officer ordering me: *'Wewe kuja hapa'*, he shouted. The man was in plain clothes and was holding a walkie-talkie. *'Kuja hapa, ona tupa nini kwa maji? Si wewe ona tupa bunduki?'* He enquired. All this meant that 'you come here, what have you dropped in the water' Is it not a gun?' I then realised that providence had decided otherwise, I could no longer proceed to my sanctuary across the channel as I had anticipated. So I turned back to where the man was calling. As I approached, he said to me again in Swahili '*Kuja saidia sisi, beba muntu hii!*' meaning 'come and assist us carry this person, 'I did not know what was wrong with the man he wanted me to help them carry, but I followed him. I later realised that the man I was to assist carrying was the dead body I saw sprawled across the shop entrance and it was of a young man who I had known. This young man had been one of the many who earned their living from commissions received on the sale of used tyres. He had been hit by a bullet through the face, coming out at the back of the head and, on close examination, I discovered another bullet had hit him at the stomach, blasting through the spinal cord at the back. He must have died instantly! This then was my assignment! I handed my identity cards which were in the front pocket of my shirt, to the security man who had called me, imploring him to keep them safe for me till I completed the job.

There was another man who was to help me load the corpse into the boot of a dirty-yellow 12Y Toyota Saloon vehicle, which was at hand. I would like to inform the reader that though this was a gruelling task for me, it was not the first time I was faced with the task of carrying a bullet ridden corpse. I had been initiated in this business at the demise of my dear uncle, who had been shot at his home at Namirembe during the rule of the military commission in 1980. I therefore proceeded, courteously. One of the security personnel shouted at me again in Swahili 'onagopa nini?' he asked. '*wewe beba haraka onagopa nini mbona huyo ali kua mzima sasawa wewe, pengine nawewe onaweza kumfata!*' Meaning 'What are you afraid of? Lift the body quickly what are you afraid of; moreover that man was also alive like you are' "You can also follow him you know!" I was shocked and stunned by the man's utterance and realised that unless my creator rescued me from this predicament, I was also dead meat. I did not answer back but went about the business as well as I could only mumbling to my colleague to hurry up so we could finish the job! The corpse couldn't be fitted into the boot of the car as it was already stiff! Moreover even in life the young man had been tall. We communicated our findings to the security men around and they then decided that it would then have to be taken in the back seat of the vehicle. A canvas to cover the seat, from the blood oozing out of the corpse was sought and got, and was spread out on the seat before we proceeded to ferry the corpse into the back of the car. I well remember we managed to do the job but it had not been an easy task!

Having accomplished the task of lifting in the dead body, we knew that everything was over till one man, who happened to be one of the group of security operatives at hand, inquired in Swahili *'Nani ata sindekereza maiti hi?'* meaning 'Who is going to escort the corpse? My heart missed a beat. I asked myself why it was necessary to accompany the dead body and to where?' When it dawned on me what the implication of that statement was, I thought hard and immediately sought for a way out of this situation. 'I have to disappear from here' I said to myself. Then I remembered it was not going to be easy as my identity papers were with one of these people! All the same I started sneaking away from the scene, towards where some abandoned water carrying jerrycans, belonging to car washers were. As I was about to reach them, the soldier I had entrusted with my documents called and asked me to go for them saying in Swahili *'kamaata bitamburisho byako'* meaning 'Come and get your identity cards.' I went to him and requested him to kindly put them in my trousers back' pocket, pointing out that I could not do so myself as my shirt front and trousers plus both my hands were full of blood. He obliged. If at that time someone who knew me had seen me in that state he could have thought I had turned into a butcher. The man then told me to go and clean myself and leave the place immediately continuing in Swahili he said *'kwenda zako tutapata wengine ambao watatusaidia kusendekereza maiti osi jali.'* Meaning 'Go well we shall get others to accompany the dead body,' On impulse I shot off, running like a man being chased by the devil himself. I went towards the back of remand prison, on to Kyaggwe Road, and back to Mackay Road to once again join my colleagues, thanking God for my narrow escape from escorting a corpse to where I knew not!

14
Walking Chimney's Legacy
Julius Ocwinyo

Our fear of him was deep and our respect total. And when we heard that he had dared fight and hurt three tough military policemen, we firmly placed him among our greatest heroes. He was our teacher, and Walking Chimney was his nickname.

Walking Chimney was the most awesome physics teacher in Lango, and possibly in the whole of Uganda. He was a strapping six-foot-two and was endowed with a deep voice and a broad chest, and he had the narrowest waist you've ever seen on a man. He had been a student at Namilyango College, and in his boxing career there and elsewhere later he had knocked out enough teeth to fill a palm-leaf basket – or so it was rumoured. A story was told of how, before his transfer to Lango College, Lira, Walking Chimney had picked up a particularly unruly senior four student by his shirt collar and the waistband of his restless khaki shorts and flung him out of the window. Nobody established which school this incident had taken place in, but just looking at Walking Chimney's tall menacing frame made one believe implicitly that he had done it.

Walking Chimney was just that – he was a smoke-spewing chimney that happened to possess a pair of legs. As a smoker he was an over-achiever: he worked through four packets of cigarettes a day. And he did not seem to be very particular about brands; he would smoke whichever brand he could afford at any one particular moment. If anyone cared enough to warn him about the dangers of smoking, and especially of mixing cigarette brands, he would give them one standard answer: THEY COULD GO TELL THEIR OWN MOTHERS THAT.

But this time round Walking Chimney had overreached himself. He had imbibed one korokoro of millet beer, and with the fumes of the beverages swirling around inside his skull, he had strutted over to a bar where he was certain to find military policemen – Red Tops, as we referred to them on account of their red-topped caps. Walking Chimney had provoked a fight that had seen one Red Top lose two upper teeth, another sustain three dislocated ribs and a third, a swollen eye. Walking Chimney himself had sustained bruises all over his body and acquired a big lump on his head which he carried around like a beacon of great courage. If he had drawn the line at that, the school community would not have been so worried and frightened. But Walking Chimney had done more. He had grabbed a G3 sub-machine gun from one of the Red- Top and had sped away into the darkness amid gunshots. He arrived at the Lango College football pitch, proudly named The Pacific because of its size, and had dumped the gun there. He had then fled to Kampala on a night bus.

Few students had dared sleep in the dormitories in the next few days though the Red Tops had recovered their gun the day after it had been grabbed from them. The year was 1977, the month was February, and the national president was Idi Amin.

'I told you these soldiers would bide their time, and then they would strike,' Okae said 'when everyone had forgotten.'

What did you expect them to do? To strike when they knew only few students would be sleeping in the dormitories?' Alyau mocked.

'Did you think they would forget the humiliation they suffered at Walking Chimney's hands?'

The news of the 'intended' invasion of Lango College by the local military police contingent spread around the school with the speed of a bushfire. Since Walking Chimneys foolhardy adventure, the students had been constantly on tenterhooks. Two incidents that day had 'confirmed' their suspicion that the military intended to attack the school. The first incident was when many of the students thought to have friends and relatives among the local soldiers could not be seen around the school by late afternoon. The second incident was reported by a drunken student. On his way back to school from drinking arege, the local gin, the student had spotted what he firmly believed was a Uganda Army Land Rover parked at Shan Ali's garage, situated a few meters away from Lango College. He had also seen two soldiers leaning against the Land Rover. According to this student, one of the soldiers, while waving his arms in the general direction of Lango College, had said '*Hapa yote*' which the student interpreted to mean 'we shall kill them all'. The drunken student had noticed all this by 8.00pm.

'But do we have to be punished for Walking Chimney's folly?' asked Okae. 'OK, if they want him that badly, then they had better follow him to Kampala and get hold of him!'

'Do you think Kampala is like Tee-Lela village where everybody knows everybody else?' Alyau retorted. Why don't you go there and try to trace Walking Chimney yourself?'

'I thought it was not so difficult to find someone in the city,' Okae, the rural boy, lamely remarked.

The moment night fell on the day, everyone felt they owed it to themselves to stay awake till morning. But sleep happens to be such a warmly seductive and sneaky thing. When it happened, therefore, everyone was firmly nestled in the bosom of sleep. It was Ochilo's night-shattering shriek and silent flight down the upstairs corridor of Odora House that triggered the stampede.

When I woke and sat up, all I could hear was the sound of pounding feet and creaking beds. Not a single other sound. As my eyes got used to the darkness, I began to notice shapes fleeing past the foot of my ground-floor bed. I leapt up amid a great creaking of my spring bed and sped after my dormitory mates.

My heart pounded wildly as I raced across the grassy space between my dormitory, Brown House, and the school cassava garden which also served as one of the boundaries of the school. I plunged into the cassava garden, my throat constricted with fright. There were shapes in flight everywhere. The feet of the running students broke in fragile cassava stems, with sharp, snapping sounds. I tripped over the stems several times, stumbled and fell two or three times, but I pressed on until I cleared the cassava garden. I ran even faster then, pounding past the ghostly shapes of cone-shaped, grass-thatched huts, oblong mabati houses, through many village paths, maize gardens, sweet potato gardens, other cassava gardens, following the direction that those ahead of me took. When we reached a large cotton field, we decided that we had done enough running for the night and that nobody, however determined they were to kill us, would follow us up to the cotton field. So we settled down in that field for the night.

There was a grand total of four bed sheets among the more than fifty of us. I had stripped down to my blue-and-red pants for bed since I had thought that all the talk about the soldiers intending to invade our school was nothing but hot air. I still wonder where I would have found the courage to walk back to school in brief pants alone. Fortunately for me I happened to have been one of those who carried a bed sheet along.

Well, it was not exactly intentional, the bed sheet just seemed to have stuck to my arm as I jumped up and rushed out of the dormitory. As a result of the severe shortage of bed sheets in the cotton field, I had to share mine with three students, laying it across our stomachs to try and prevent bellyaches occasioned by the cold.

We were startled out of our sleep at around 5.00 am. when one of us who had woken up a few minutes earlier saw a crouching figure moving cautiously in our direction. The figure came from the direction of a stream that followed some one hundred meters away from the cotton field. Our friend wasn't quite sure he had seen right, so he sat up, rubbed his eyes, and looked again, harder. Then he screamed out one single word: '*KEYA!*' SOLDIER! And then he leapt up and sped away.

We all scrambled up and were off in a flash. We found ourselves instinctively running back to our school. We did not have quite as much stamina as we had possessed on our way out of the school. The result was that this time around we could not reach the high speeds we had achieved earlier. The crouching figure, tenacious like an evil spirit, stumbled along after us. He looked like a man holding out something long in front of him. We thought it was a gun.

We ran on. The 'soldier' kept pace with us. But no shots rang out. Instead he seemed to be calling out to us. In Luo.

Still we ran – until we reached the home of a man called Orombi. Then we called a halt. We stood around, packed tightly together like frightened goats, and just as alert, waiting for the 'soldier' to arrive.

He turned out to be Amol, a senior three student. He was so tired he couldn't stand. So he plumped down. Right there on the dew-covered grass in Orombi's compound. And his breath came in sharp, painful gasps.

'Look,' he gasped, 'I-I-thought you-would-recognise me-and then wait-for me'.

We had wanted to beat him up for scaring us so badly, but now began to pity him. One of us asked him what had happened to him.

'What happened?' he said 'Well-you know that-that stream near the-the ginnery.' He was referring to Odokomit Ginnery. 'Well, I got into that stream-went in up to-up to my neck. And there were all these-these mosquitoes-whole swarms of them-attacking me like-like I had done them some-some wrong-but I could not hit them-what-if-if someone heard?'

We laughed at him now.

He went on: 'And then something came-wriggling on the surface-of the water. Something long-black-and shiny, glistening-I think it was a snake-I leapt out of the water-and ran.'

We laughed again, stealthily though for we were still rather frightened. We did not believe Amol about the snake. We thought the snake was a figment of Amol's fright-sharpened imagination.

We trooped back into school at the break of dawn, with me draped like a Turkana maiden in a light green bed sheet. Some of the casualties of the previous night's stampede were getting into the school truck – a cream – coloured Toyota Hiace - to be taken to hospital. There were no serious injuries. Some sprains, bruises, cuts, bumps and broken heads, but no broken bones.

It was later established that Ochilo, the Senior two student who had caused the stampede, had been dreaming. He had been dreaming that the three Red Tops that Walking Chimney had fought, had caught him and tied him to the trunk of an opok tree. Now one of them was sharpening his sparkling knife on a large stone in readiness to slash his throat. That was when Ochilo had screamed.

15
The Last of the Jungle Foxes

Olupot James Peter Egoing

It was a Wednesday, the 9th day of March 1994. We had bivouacked in the early hours of the day in a small thicket near Kanyum Primary School. At around 5.30 am. I woke up to tie my belongings before lying down and pillowing them. Already two lookouts were perched in the tree we lay under.

It appears I fell asleep again for I was rudely woken up by the sound of objects crashing through the branches and landing with two thuds. That spelled close danger. Our immediate impulse was to grab our guns, and then run away. Like the rest, I scrambled up and ran in the direction taken by the two men who had fallen from their observation posts. After about two hundred meters, we stopped to analyse the danger. It was soldiers all right. The direction of approach and reaction suggested they had not known we were there, but had just been attracted by our running.

A brief glance told us that the soldiers, who were now firing, slightly outnumbered us. We were seven, the last of UPA rebels in the field.

Seven years back we were just part of the thousands of rebels who fought the government. There were other groups. Our front's leaders were said to be overseas, and we never saw them for the duration of the war.

In the insurgency's heyday, the local commanders would urge the boys to fight on, and never to surrender. Indeed they did fight, losing their comrades and never making good their losses. Some boys fought exceptionally well, better indeed than trained men.

Seven years on, the majority of the officers and men of the once mighty rebel force had surrendered, run away, or as happened to some, including the most prominent ones in our zone, Lt. Willy Okotel and Lt. Nathan Akure (brother to the author), preferred to die 'honorably' than otherwise.

We were always bitter at those colleagues who had chosen to surrender, or even betray us. Whenever we came across any such, it never fared well for him. The greater our desperation, the more vicious we could be.

By now, we were only seven officers and men, the last of the great force in the whole district and perhaps in the whole former operation zones of UPA, no longer fighting for anybody, but only to be alive. For some time, we were able to meander in parts of the district, travelling mostly at night and hiding during the day, to avoid the numerous military detachments scattered all over the district. Occasionally, we would pronounce our presence.

This Wednesday morning, our number notwithstanding, we went at these soldiers who had disrupted our sleep. A few shots, weird yells, and they were obliged to break ground. We briefly pursued them, sent a few more shots their way and then returned jubilantly to pack our bags.

'Even bean eaters trying to scare us...'

'Why arouse our fighting appetite and then run away...?'

When everybody had their bags on, the leader looked at me.

'This is your zone. Now what?'

'I suggested we enter the same thickets they did, but a little to the left. Those children are still full of running steam and may now be miles away. We can sneak our way out and to Kamacha, and from there, out-maneuver any follow-up.'

'No,' the leader objected. 'We have just come from that direction and should not go back. Our objective was Ngora, and it still is. We ought to cross over there.'

'In this broad daylight?' I asked incredulously.

'What matters is crossing the main (Kanyum - Mukongoro) road.'

I looked at him askance, then around for other opinions. Finding none, I turned, held my gun ready and led the way. I intended to cross the main road as close to Kanyum trading center as possible. Most of the soldiers there must have gone out on their daily operations.

We had covered about 500 meters when I heard someone down the line asking who those people were, I looked back at the speaker and followed his eyes to our right. Some persons were cautiously coming towards us, peering ahead as they did so. They were armed, and could only be soldiers from Kanyum barracks, a little over a kilometer away.

When I waved my cap above my head, and there was no response from them, I realised the ruse had failed. From the corner of my eye, I saw my colleagues turn and run. I had scarcely turned when the attack started. The chase had begun. A little further on, I passed some luggage thrown away by my colleagues to make themselves lighter.

We ran and crossed the road at the primary school, with the posse hard on us. The young ones among us were nimble and fast. The rest of us fell behind. We occasionally stopped to fire back running to catch up with our colleagues who knew how to live longer.

A little later, the fastest of our colleagues ran back, past us and away to the left. Looking out from the edge of the thicket, way ahead I saw another group of soldiers, fanning out and coming towards the gunfire, cautiously but deliberately. We change course, running now towards Kanyum sub-county headquarters. For a short while, the posse seemed to lose track of us, and so we held our fire for fear of giving away our position. But just as it seemed we had escaped, they appeared again.

The situation seemed desperate, we were being maneuvered towards the barracks. But we had an ace left, a rifle launched grenade (TNT). It was fixed and fired. All our eyes followed it on its cruising journey, our hopes rising as we waited for it to explode so that we could follow it with a daring charge. It landed but failed to go off.

With the last chance gone, fear lent us wings. When I called out to the others to wait, nobody appeared to hear, but when I called out to them not to be fools but avoid entering the barracks, which was 'directly under those eucalyptus', they veered to our left. We re-crossed the main road to Kanyum Senior Secondary School just under one kilometer away from the barracks. We crossed where we started from and onwards to the deep village now. We wheeled to our right into a smallwood, just short of another government detachment at Kogili.

The posse never fired while we traversed the woods. We walked most of it, and were able to recover our breath. We ran again to try to cross the main (Kanyum - Makongoro) road, this time far from Kanyum.

Alas, as we came out of the woods, we met a new threat. The posse had merely skirted the woods and now strove to head us off the main road. A brief exchange ensued, and they fell behind us, not two hundred meters, and on bare terrain!

We raced to cross the bare ground. Again from ahead, my faster colleagues ran back. At the main road, some three hundred meters ahead, I saw a sparse line of soldiers. They must have imagined that just the sight of their imposing appearance would scare us. No. In any case, we had nowhere to turn, as even the dazed speedoholics realised the posse at the rear and on the flanks was too close for comfort.

A colleague beside me broke down. A while back I had urged him to carry on when he complained his head was spinning. He was a good fellow, better fitted to be a priest than a soldier. John Ogagul (RIP), he was the division administrator.

A few weeks back, he was bathing when soldiers attacked us at night. In his haste to scramble away, most of his arsenal of Botano-chemistry protection was lost. That only served to strengthen my resolve never to remove clothing from my body, even for the love of bathing. The clothes shone with dirt. What mattered was being alive and alert.

Of late he was constantly worried and feared for his security.

'James, I am collapsing.' He now gasped.

I asked him to raise his head to look how close the posse was. The last I saw of him, he was dropping to his knees and gently falling on his left. The posse, which hovered but forty meters back, called on him to drop his gun and surrender. Looking around, I realised that we were now almost surrounded, and was mad at it. Were we going to be caught just like 'wet hens' No, not me.

I rallied two of our milling boys, shoved one to the left and sent the other off to the right. I took the center, and together, we stormed our way forward. At no other time have I fought with such tenacity, willing to die one way or the other, fighting, but not to surrender.

'Fire and maneuver.' I urged the two boys. We have to cross or die in the attempt.'

When they realised that we were not going to turn away, the soldiers took cover and fought back, but were brushed off by our daring charge. I remember holding my gun in my left hand, standing in the middle of the road, as I surveyed both ways. The two boys were foolhardly running at the soldiers. A soldier to my right remembered courage and fired at me behind an anthill about one hundred meters away. I jabbed a finger at him, and when he would not run away, I made at him, and he scrambled off.

This fight taught me never to force an opponent into a situation where he feels utterly desperate. He will fight with tenacity, knowing that he has no other choice.

We crossed, and the last of the soldiers rallied to take over the chase while the former came up after. A little further on, and we were fired on again from a cluster of huts, which described a detachment. We veered away again from a cluster of back. I became aware of the proximity of the posse. I turned round, took aim and fired. I saw a few soldiers rush to help one, while the rest scattered.

The incident gave me time to walk on a fair distance and recover my breath. I had long since ceased calling to the others to wait. It was now everyone for himself, and a colleague's demise at the rear benefited the others by delaying the posse and giving them time to cover more ground.

Eventually I caught up with them, and together we walked on. We were even beginning to snigger at another close shave, when we saw another group of soldiers trotting to cross our path at right angles. We showed no apprehension, and they may have been confused about who this small group in mixed fatigues was. Some of them crossed while those at the back stopped. Our leader bellowed at them in proper military voice.

'Don't just stand there, run across after them there.' He jabbed a finger to our left.

'Don't shoot.' He whispered back up our line.

Several soldiers obeyed. The rest stayed up, rifles on their shoulders, 30 meters, 20, 15 Jesus! Were we going to shake hands or? Timely enough, the posse caught up and now let loose at all of us. We ran together, neck and neck. While we the rebels carried on, the group wheeled to the left after their comrades who had crossed the road. One or two from our group stopped to fire at the soldiers descending the slope.

I again fell back as we ran. My chest was fit to burst, and I began losing interest in everything – pushing my chest, running to catch up with the comrades who would again bust forth, and even in life itself. I started taking my last glimpses of mother earth. I was not oblivious of the soldiers who were now but a stone's throw away, but I no longer cared. When they fired, I felt the bursts as if in my head.

'God grant that it be a necker.' I muttered. I did not want to be taken alive, even wounded. I shouted an obscenity as they clamored for me, my gun and especially the bag on my back. I tuned again to fire, but the bullet just kicked dust ahead from me. If it were regular soldiers, they would have fallen for cover, but the mere sight of a gun did not cow these former comrades who had surrendered, been absorbed in the Local Defence Force and turned round to hunt us. They would just duck while running on. They also still had their charms to rely on. I tried a second shot, but the gun clicked dry – no more ammo.

The intelligent part of my mind took over. I ran a few steps, jumped off the main road, and while slightly visible, pretended to change a magazine. I jumped back on the road, and feigned to shoot. They dived for cover now. Crazy, they were so near they could have sneaked out, and caught me.

I crossed over to deep thickets, frenziedly aware that I had used up my last bullet, which should have been for me! I caught up with my colleagues again and asked for ammunition. Only one of the boys had, but I failed to catch up with him, and nor would he stop to hand them over. The thickets behind had by then swallowed the posse.

Well ahead again, we espied another group, patiently awaiting their share of the game. The boy stopped and exchanged guns with me.

God, I mused, is there any getting out of this situation today? The bean eaters had the day, and we had opted to run away from them. Out of fear? No, no way, not out of it, but full fighting spirit. We had to save ourselves for another day.

We veered again to the right, now making a semicircle around Kanyum. At this point, I told my colleagues that we should charge at the Kanyum market, fire to create chaos, and melt out with the civilians in the market. No response.

Crossing a dried up swamp, a couple of bullets kicked up dust just by our feet. We looked back to see a larger and better armed force coming at us from the opposite side, about eight hundred meters away. We also realised that another comrade was missing.

I was so tired. I looked down at my body and decided the belt had to go. Someone suggested that I throw my bag as well, to lighten myself. I refused. I would die with it I replied.

There was a thicket to be crossed before reaching Aukot primary school. I announced that I could no longer go further, but would hide here.

'Come with us a bit, and as we enter deeper, you can branch in and hide, but remember where we shall meet in Ngora.'

'I know.' I said. I paused to let them go without knowing which way I took, then turned in. I found in some thorny thicket a hole long ago bored into a hill probably by some hunters, and I settled in there. I was completely soaked with perspiration, even my nails appeared to sweat.

A minute later bunches of posse swept past. I watched them panting along wondering at 'what kind of persons these were, who don't tire, even with fresher posses taking over the chase'.

My clothes let off a strong odour. Crazy, couldn't they realise it? They must have stunk, themselves, I thought. I could have killed a few if I let loose at them. However, the spirit of suicide did not appeal to me.

A little later, bursts of automatic gunfire told me that my colleagues were now at the main (Kanyum - Kumi) road. My passing friends were jubilant, and talked of those 'bad people falling into an ambush'. When the firing retrogressed, I hoped my comrades had crossed, though I feared a worse outcome.

The last of the posse filed past. Less than twenty minutes later, I heard more gunfire bursts, faintly this time.

Later still, I heard ululation, and then a speeding vehicle. It only meant that one of our colleagues had been killed and was being sped to the district headquarters for public spectacle. Who could it have been?

Subsequently, I began hearing voices of the civilians coming back from market. They were talking excitedly of the killing of? I strained my ear well. Abwongoto. Oh alas, God rest his soul for a former comrade, I muttered. He was our leader. A former qualified teacher, he had fallen in with the rebellion and was, at the time, our division commander with only six officers and men to his division.

'Any one else' I strained my ears to listen.

'They say even Egoing has a broken leg and is hiding in a thicket somewhere. They are going to comb him out also.'

I winced at that mention of my name. Could it be that one of our boys had been captured and had talked?

'At least now that they have routed those people, we can start rearing chicken.' 'They say another one was captured but killed at the main road to Mukongoro.' 'Much if they had killed them all.'

'That they also shot two soldiers, but they have been taken to Atutur Hospital.'

Not wanting to spend the whole morning eaves-dropping there, I had to think and act fast. Now that Abwongoto, then Ogagul were dead and another was missing, where should I start? Shouldn't I wait for night fall to hear the details, before taking any necessary move? I couldn't cross to Ngora without knowing the fate of the rest of my colleagues. I might wander there, but fall into a trap.

For now, I ruled out the issue of surrender in view of all that I heard. All the same, should I stay here on our tracks and risk being discovered?

I felt my body begin to relax, and I became lost in deep thought and even forgot how I fell asleep.

However, a couple of hours later I emerged from my hiding place, and watched in unconcealed amusement at the army officers who stepped forward cautiously, well behind the bolder Members of Parliament and Local Councillors (By then NRC members and RCs) as they approached me. I wish I could join the officers momentarily in the contemplation of myself, maybe I would realise why they stared at me so.

I was willing to surrender, I told them after the preliminaries, if the Presidential Amnesty and Pardon was still in place. And if not, I requested to be shot, there and then, and my people to be allowed to take my body for burial, without ado. I felt ashamed, as if my dead comrades were watching me.

When they heard of it, the soldiers in Kanyum felt cheated by a different unit picking me up from right under their noses, and blamed the Local Councillors for having fetched the officers from a distant barracks when they were just under a kilometer from where I hid.

16
A Narrow Escape from God's Soldiers
Oola Patrick Lumumba

No sooner had I played my master card than Kidega, one of my friends who was standing outside the small grass thatched house in Alero Sub-County, shouted 'Soldiers! Soldiers!' That one was on the cloudy afternoon of Thursday 27th May 1995, a day before the national mourning day for Atyiak victims (of Gulu) who were massacred in cold blood by the Lord's Resistance Army (LRA) commanded by Otii Lagony, Kony's first in command.

'Don't run, don't run you are all under arrest.' One of the soldiers shouted at us from the door entrance, pointing the barrel of his gun straight at us. But Kidega who was already out of the house took to his heels leaving his shirt in the hands of the rebels.

'Get out quickly,' the man barked at us and we did so. He asked us if we had heard of the Atyak incident and we answered him affirmatively. He then told us that we are going to be birds of the same feathers. He asked my age I told him I was fourteen (although I was seventeenth). He ordered that my hands be tied up and it was done in a couple of seconds, hands backwards and elbow to elbow (kandoya).

My friends, Ojok and Onen were laid down facing the sun, waiting for bayonets. Their sin was that they were mature and above age (14 years). While Opira (age about 8) was ordered to catch hens by Captain Lagira. He was putting on full army uniform with a heavy black coat like that of Uganda Securiko of these days, the hot weather notwithstanding. He also ordered for the destruction of Kidega's bicycle which he had left behind laid against the wall of the hut we were playing cards in. Within few minutes, an axe was at work.

'Sir, let me help in finishing these ones,' one of the rebels who came running shouted at the top of his voice, brandishing the bayonet of his gun. But Lagira told him that there would be no killing there.

Shortly, an order came from the most high teacher Mr. Otii Lagony who was leading the group of about 120-150 soldiers including abductees. He said people should hurry up to join the line which was just about 100 meters only on the path leading to Alero Trading Center.

We joined them. They were all squatting as if they were poised for an ambush. We started to head for the trading center as it started raining. There was dead silence in the group as we moved but only to be interrupted by loud cries of a certain boy (age about 11) who was from the cattle fair at the trading center. He was unfortunate to have met the rebels on his way back home. He was protesting being abducted, saying that he was the only child of his widowed mother, a victim of leprosy who lived all alone at home. But none of that made any impression on the Lord's Army who only pulled their pangas for the poor boy prompting him to agree with them immediately. He too was tied kandoya.

Suddenly an order came from above that all those who were carrying 'good' guns like RPG, LMG, anti-tanks and mortars should lead the line since we were now approaching the centre. And within a minute the 'best' boys and girls were in front leading the group with one of the commanders carrying an LMG and his escort carrying the bullets in a fertiliser bag. All the soldiers started wearing 'red' eyes including the young girls whose number was nearly as many as the boys.

'Branch from here and start making the line quickly. We are time barred,' The king ordered just as the site of the UPDF detach became clearly seen. The line was made roughly 300 meters from the round grass-thatched army barracks situated in an enclosure that was clear of trees and tall grasses. Trouble, however, came when the pain from the chest (kandoya) became too much after the long journey of about eight miles to the center and my humble request to one of the rebels (age about 11, to untie me a bit.

'*Jau I waci ngo? I mito ni dong agony toli wek ingwec oko?*' (He replied to me in Acholi meaning that I now wanted my rope be untied so that I ran away.) He then accused me of trying to show a bad example to other prisoners and drew his panga for my neck as well as drawing the attention of others. I held my breath, looked at the boy and told him that he hadn't understood me. I told him that I have begged him to pull down my shorts so that I ease myself (urinate) but not what he was saying.

'You mean you can't do that on your body?' a girl asked me. She started convincing the boy that they should not spare me. This would show the other prisoners the kind of people they were. But God intervened and no sooner had they started killing me than they started getting strokes from one of their commanders who wanted the line filled quickly so that the play begins. I held my breath as they hurried to the front line and glorified God in my heart.

Immediately I heard a gunshot from the LRA chief commander Mr Lagony who was just holding an AK47, ordering fire to begin. Thousands of abuses and insults issued from the Lord's soldiers to Uganda Peoples Defence Force. The insults are too black to mention here as most of them concerned the private parts of the enemies mothers. The girls in the front which was just some 100 meters from us were also inviting their enemies (UPDF) for sex, claiming that they are more than ready. UPDF on the other hand were all in dead silence, waiting for orders from their captain as they aimed their guns not to miss the targets.

'Fire-re-re', the UPDF commander shouted at the top of his voice, firing about three bullets from his pistol into air. In just a couple of seconds the air was full of flying bombs on either side, followed by 'rains' of bullets.

Yes, the 'play' had started. Gunshots were rocking the air to the maximum and the abuses ceased very quickly. I could see the tall elephant grass, sugarcane and tree branches suffering like nothing. One could also hear people crying 'ma ato' (mother I am dead) very clearly, leave alone seeing others falling abruptly as if they were drunk especially the LRA whose battle tactics forbade them from taking cover. Twekwene was shot just about one meter away from me and yet we were behind the front line.

The first round of firing lasted about 45 minutes. Only to be diluted with occasional exchange of shooting. This took about 10 minutes before the second round suddenly rocked in. It started again by mostly exchange of bombs and other guns followed.

But shortly after, chaos ensued among Kony soldiers as a gas bomb was reportedly being shot by the UPDF. More reinforcement was called in by the so called teachers and I saw young boys and girls running like mad dogs to join the battle other than dying behind. The fighting became very intensive. This lasted for about 35 minutes. That was the second round. Time was about 6.00 pm.

The last round started in a very boring fashion as is always the case in many things. No shouting or morale boosting. But suddenly, after a period of about 30 minutes, things turned to be very sweet just like one could enjoy the end of sugarcane. This however was only on the side of the Lords Resistance Army (LRA). They started shouting '*mak amaka*' in Acholi meaning 'catch them alive'. There was also shouting in Kiswahili probably from some UPDF begging for mercy. They (LRA) had won the war although with a good number of casualties.

Immediately, I started seeing people very busy, moving up and down looting the barracks. A pregnant woman carrying a baby on her back (probably a wife of a UPDF soldier) was forced to carry about six guns but was later set free. Everybody was coming back from the barracks very victoriously, holding two to three excess guns. But this was short lived.

Just as they had started burning the huts in the barracks, a helicopter gunship with either doors wide open came at a terrible speed not too high from the ground level. Gun firing started rocking from it very intensively up to the extent that the guns barrel could sometimes become red like an iron being melted. Everybody took cover in different directions under the bushes. It was already becoming dark and the gunship went back very shortly thereafter.

I was untied and given about six pieces of luggage to carry including six anti-tank shells. I did so. My boss asked me if I had ever been a soldier. I denied but he told me to be fearless.

We crossed the stream very quickly, retreating to the direction from which we had come, but they later took other directions. It was already so dark that the commanders could only lead the way with flashing torches. My boss gave me an army pair of trousers, gum boots and a heavy jacket for my comfort as we pathed our way in the bushes.

But trouble again came in when a young girl (age about 13), started complaining very bitterly about the violation of their rules.

'How can this boy be dressed like this so soon and yet he is still a very new abductee who hasn't stayed here for at least a period of two weeks?' She complained to other commanders adding that I was also above age (14 years). She was putting on a heavily blood stained army shirt since she had been helping a wounded friend from the front line although in vain. The friend kicked the bucket.

'But he is still very young and even fitting you exactly. I wish he lives for you.' My boss who looked very friendly backed me. The girl doubted with a shake of her head but with some sweet smiles on her face, only to get sad again all of a sudden. She might have remembered her lost friend.

At around 9.00 pm., we were already busy raiding chickens for food. We could hear some of the UPDF who had escaped from the war coming back to their barracks with some heavy firing again as if the war had just started only to find their now looted barracks empty.

We got settled at around 1.00 am. in an open bush some far distance from Alero trading center where the fighting took place. It was quite cold.

We started cooking immediately. For us of Kilwa Company (a group of about seven) there were four big chickens. I helped the escorts to mingle posho since Esther (age about 16 and wife to my boss) was tired from the 'march'. The other escort 'Kwene' a nickname in Acholi meaning 'where is he' was injured in the chest. The bullet which was still inside his flesh was even removed from there using an old razor blade. He was later given PPF injections of 5mm by the highly 'qualified' nurse whose qualification I later learnt was primary six. She was called Rose.

My teacher brought some local cooking oil called 'moo ya' in Acholi and anointed me among other new abductees to officially become their soldiers. The oil was put on our forehead, followed by chest then back, tracing the sign of the cross after a brief prayer led by him.

Another problem, however, arose when I took food to him (my boss) who was by then in the headquarters together with his friends except the semi-god, Mr. Otii Lagony and Lagira. I made a very big offence by glancing at one of the UPDF so-called secret letters they were reading.

'Young boy, get seated immediately, One of them ordered me with a flashlight shone straight on my eyes. I received a couple of slaps on my cheek. Tears rolled freely from my cheeks and I could hardly control them from pouring down. The man accused me of stealing their secrets.

Young people: today I have become to believe that we are really God's soldiers. May he who has brought us from Sudan grant us more victories and a peaceful stay in Uganda. He glorified God and asked me if I am not the one call Pat (derived from Patrick). I answered yes. He asked who my boss and I revealed to him.

Sir, he is lucky to have stayed this long but it's not yet too late. I will tell you his life history later, he told my master who only held a deep breath. He continued accusing me of having been a UPDF intelligence officer, an opium taker and that I have deliberately refused to study. He concluded by passing a death sentence upon me lest I escape with their guns. By now all the 'lions' eyes were fixed on me but in dead silence as they waited for my master's decisions. I was busy offering my last prayers to God.

But all of a sudden, the accuser blundered by asking me to defend myself. I held my breath and boldly told him that I was a Roman Catholic and my religion forbade opium smoking. I had never linked myself to NRA/UPDF in my life and my dropping out of school (yet I was an S.3 student) was due to poverty. That I pledged to serve them up to the end.

'You have saved yourself with your wise words. But any attempt to escape will prompt destruction of all your clan people.' He warned me and asked if my mother is still in her petty business in fish before he dismissed me from the group after introducing himself as Oola. I answered affirmatively and gave them the food I had taken.

My friend Tye Kwene was shocked. He told me that God is really with me because my case was too strong compared to very many people they had executed. I should then just be patient and wait to enjoy ranks and wives especially if I am active.

Immediately, my friend Alex was called for an interview and 'Tye Kwene confided to me that the boy is going to be killed that night if not early in the morning. His sin was that he was big. Alex was about 25 years and was picked at around 5.00 am. by the so called Oola who first mistook me for Alex. On realising his error he told me to continue sleeping. He led him to a distance of about ten meters and in no minute, the poor handsome boy was crying at the top of his voice that he was dying innocently as the man stabbed him with his bayonet. May God bless his soul.

That morning at around 7.00 am another spate of fighting broke out again between the rebels and the UPDF militia. It was brief since the militia met us so abruptly and were only shooting covering fire as they retreated to organise themselves. I saw no death and that one was at a place called Got Moko.

From around 10.00 am to nearly midday we were in trouble again from helicopter attack. I came to learn that God was directly handling me from here. This was when the gunship *(sura Mbaya)* got me in a bare place and the pilot had to turn directly for me. I was ordered just to sit there on that spot lest the helicopter came for other people as it might follow me. I threw myself on the ground and held my head with my hands as I waited for one of the thousands of bullets rocking the soil around me to hit my back.

'Take off your jacket, throw it away to confuse the pilot and let that white jerrycan of yours get hidden'. One of the sympathisers, in fact, the young girl who was yesterday putting on the blood stained shirt, shouted from her hiding place as others were just busy enjoying the scene. The trick worked and the gunship changed direction after nearly ten minutes constant firing at me. I was sweating profusely and everybody was amused how I escaped those thousands of bullets. May the young girl live longer.

To cut the story short, how then did I manage to escape? It was from that evening of Friday 28th May 1995 that I made my way from a place called Amuro Mutema, some 40Km west of Gulu town and deep in the village where the people lived in inherent poverty.

By then I was very tired and Esther had already told me that Lagony had already ordered my death because my jerrycan was knocking here and there when we were crossing Amuro road, something which was forbidden to them since it is an act of directly calling their enemies (who might be on their way) to attack them. The offence was only punishable by death. I was however only to help carrying the luggage which was by then weighing almost 50Kg. Yet, we still had an unknown distance to cover, crossing the swamps and thick forests not to mention staying hungry as I waited for my minutes to come. Too much for a slave.

I raised my eyes to heaven and asked the Lord for my rescue or else grant me a peaceful death (bullets other than pangas) when all of a sudden I found myself in luck. And just after about 20 minutes, things started happening miraculously. Two helicopter gunships (sura Mbaya) were already in the air, thirsty for the LRA blood. The time has come.

The commandos in the gunships were at work. One of the helicopters was busy releasing bombs which were producing terribly black smoke and bursting into fire while the other one was in real instrumental and everybody was panicking as they took cover in different corners.

The nurse (called Rose), the most ugly woman on earth I have so far set eyes on with missing teeth which looked like an empty plot in the slum decided to distinguish herself from the line. I quickly allotted myself to be her escort and followed her.

Events however turned round when Rose learnt of my plan to escape and fixed her big nose for my chest with a bayonet in her right hand. But no sooner had she started stabbing me than the commando shooting the LMG turned the barrel of his gun straight at us and within a few minutes thousands of bullets were already rocking the groundnuts garden we were standing in. Rose took to her heels, dropping even her packages behind and I took the other direction and got hidden for good.

God had already finished his work of rescue. The helicopters ceased and I could only hear the weaver birds singing in the nearby papyrus swamps, civilians also pulling their necks from their hiding places. One was in the swamp.

The following morning the civilians took me to the UPDF in Amuru Barracks and the OC Barracks Mr. Nseriko put me in the minister's helicopter. I travelled with the former minister of state for northern Uganda Ms Betty Bigombe who was from her official visit to Amuru. She never minded my stinking body yet I had spent days without bathing.

I spent a period of about two weeks in Gulu 4th Division Barracks under good treatment and was later handed over to World Vision where I spent a period of five weeks before being officially handed over to my family members in mid-July 1995. I lived to tell the story.

17
Bloody Hours Begin

Davis Dickens Opira

After the painful loss of the most memorable battle of Corner-Kilak of 1987 between the NRA and the (HSMF) Lakwena moved with her team to Opit railway station where the altar was. There were sacrifices, prayers, initiation, and cleansing functions to the spirits to ask for reconciliation and pardon.

While at Opit railway station, Lakwena became very ruthless and the work of the operation department came to the foreground. She became unsympathetic to everybody including her personal soldiers. Army misconduct or a slight offence believed to be outside the interest of the spirits was punishable by death. Their necks were cut with a sword (panga). This was also the period when Severino Lukoya Kibero visited his daughter Alice Auma. It was the first time for people to see Lukoya in the flesh address the people on his call and the related heavenly experience.

At this period, Lakwena sent a decree to all the villages in Kitgum district. This message had the information that whoever had joined the army even for only one hour ought to report to Opit. She emphasised that anybody who had eaten army beans for at least a single day must report immediately. She earnestly warned of a disaster to come.

Earlier, many people had joined the army during the UNLA days. Many civilians also joined HSMF during the turbulent period of the Akarimojong cattle rustling in the district. There were many people of these categories in the villages since. They didn't want to continue with Lakwena after the heavy loss at Corner-Kilak. The War Mobilising Committee (WMC) and co-ordinators used to call for village meetings, assemblies and other public rallies to address this issue. They talked to people in churches, markets and schools and urged the persons concerned to make haste and report. The message was ignored by many people who had a diehard misconception that a soldier could not kill his subordinate who would support and reinforce him at war. Some people reported on sight of danger.

One day, Lakwena performed formal cleansing rites and blessed her operations troops. For the first time in history sent them on mission. They took off from Opit railway station and went east. They had the instruction to cross Aswa bridge at Awere and start work immediately. This operation was directed at the soldiers and other general operations were promised to be conducted later.

It occurred that a group of 'Celo-Bongo' (the common nickname for rebel fighters among local people) headed by Ongwech Leaky was stationed at Lagile. This group of looters had little regard for the HSMF because of the failure and heavy loss and were ready for any attack.

At dawn of the following day, the HSMF operation team launched a surprise attack on the 'Celo-Bongo' of Leaky. Many of this group were killed and Ongwech Leaky himself was captured and hacked to pieces. This also marked the end to the 'Celo-Bongo' thugs.

The operation team proceeded eastwards to Agago county in Kitgum district where the sorrowful bloody hours of HSMF filthy activities was heavily felt. I wish to illustrate how the bloody hours in pain were felt with two stories. The affected places were Lira-Palwo, Pajule, Pader, Achol-pii, Kalongo, Namokora, etc.

On the second day, the HSMF operation team walked quietly into Lira-Palwo division. The date for the operation was not officially declared and most people were uninformed. This enable the HSMF to accomplish a surprise capture of several young men in the area. Most of these people had worked in the UNLA, Celo-Bongo, Police or the HSMF itself.

It was indeed real ill fate for any of these captives if the path they were following passed through the forest or a quiet place. The HSMF secretly killed by beating, spearing, kniving, stoning or boxing such people. Anybody that belonged to the categories they were hunting, when not found and captured, had all his houses, granaries and everything burnt to ashes.

At Lira Palwo, the HSMF operation team captured quite a lot of people. Many of these people were secretly killed in the forest but a total of thirty eight were gathered and locked up in a small room of Lira-Palwo dispensary. The WMC and some elders came pleading for others but the HSMF operation commander told them the case would be solved the following day. They didn't show any sign of killing and everyone believed it. The news about the secret killings in the forest had not yet come up!

In the evening, the prisoners were bound up in pairs. One member of the captives, Lokol-Karim (Okello) asked his friends. 'Don't you think they will kill us?' The rest of the prisoners rebuked him sharply and retorted. 'You fool! How can a soldier kill a subordinate? They will release us soon!'

Okello-Lokol-Karim was not comforted by their remarks. Being something of a poet, he had thought over this issue with his face against the round and seen very little chance for survival. He remarked: 'How about that the houses and granaries are being burnt.'

Between eleven o'clock and mid night, the atmosphere was a dead-silence and total darkness. The people slept in their houses not very sure of what would be done to the thirty eight captives. The evening had started with rumours that there had been some secret killings done in the forest that day. Everybody was impatient for the rising sun that would bring the fulfilment the following day.

The HSMF butchers started picking the prisoners in pairs and took them to face their destiny. Okello-Lokol-Karim and Ocaya Otei were the first pair to be pulled out of that small room. Lokol-Karim had earlier whispered to Ocaya to pick out a razor blade from his hind pocket and work on the cutting of the rope in his hand. The pair did it secretly and were free but kept quiet over it.

As they walked through dark night to the sugarcane plantation to the west, Lokol-Karim and his friend broke off in a run. The executioners soon opened fire on them. Lokol escaped but Ocaya was shot dead.

'Was it successful?' asked the sentry.

The man coming back to him held a burning grass torch above his head and was panting as he answered him. 'The bigger one escaped, the smaller one did not.'

The prisoners packed in the small dispensary room were shocked by sudden gun shots, and now coupled with the conversation overheard outside, broke into a loud cry of helplessness. The knowledge had now come to them that death was their fate. The second pair was again pulled out of the room and dragged towards the same direction. One young man named Santo-Lakuc again escaped. The butchers then became disgusted and threw many grenades into the small room. The captives were killed like dogs!

In all, a total of thirty six people (corpses) were found packed in a newly-dug pit latrine at the dispensary. The HSMF operation team left the place before dawn and proceeded eastwards.

Another center of such stupid murder was Kalongo trading center. There were some UNLA groups that had returned from exile in Sudan and now wanted to join hand with friends and push the rebel war. The HSMF seduced them and the unlucky soldiers were deceived. On the evening of that same day the HSMF team disarmed them and started treating them as prisoners.

In the surrounding villages, the operation team hunting young men were deceiving the local peasants that they were going to fight in Karamoja and bring back the looted cattle. They were therefore asking for some more man power who would join them. Many stupid young men surrendered and were later secretly killed in the forest. About eighty nine people were taken and locked up in one of the classroom of Kalong Primary School.

That evening, the women of the captives took some food to their husbands but the HSMF threw that food in their faces. They were not allowed to see their husbands and others went back without knowing that their husbands had already been killed in the forest. The dark night was coming very fast and soon these captives would be dead.

As may be compared to the Biblical story of Job, at least someone would be spared to witness the message. There were two young boys who were twins. They tore their shirts into pieces, made a rope and tied it on a roof. They lifted themselves across the wall using it and jumped out on the other side and escaped. The twins were successful. The furious HSMF butchers then opened fire into the room and threw stick-grenades amidst the captives. The blood hungry men devoured the helpless captives and killed many. Some of these people were as yet only wounded.

Soon, a pretentious HSMF team intervened and entered the room quarrelling and searching for those who had fired on the captives. They summoned in the darkness those still alive but wounded to speak up so that they would give immediate medical treatment. Many of the wounded showed themselves but for that pitiful lush were finished up with swords, knives and claw hammers. A total of about eighty seven young men were killed in that classroom.

The HSMF operation team conducted such brutal operations in many villages in Kitgum district. Some young men fled the district and took asylum in the bordering district of Karamoja. This was the first bitter operation that weakened most of the people's faith in Lakwena. It was the beginning of the bloody hours of HSMF career. Sons and daughters of people died like chickens in Kitgum district.

Notes

'Celo-Bongo': This was a common nickname for the rebel fighters, Known by the indigenous people as earthly/worldly fighters. Their name meant that they were looters. It means to SHOOT, SEARCH AND LOOT **WMC** Abbreviation for War Mobilising Committee. This was the political wing backing the bush war against NRA.

18
Ambush

Oloya Okot

I sat before the community television set and I refused to believe what I was seeing. They looked like laughing giraffes - if you have ever seen one - their ears had been brutally slashed off; their lips or what remained were inseparable from the nose which was but a rather bizarre looking hole; their eye lashes and eye brows had been plucked off by an inexperienced chicken plucker; their heads were not the smooth Museveni type bald but a walking version of the scattered type of vegetation; their limbs were... I turned my face and walked away. I could not bear anymore the distorted version of a human being.

All this, as I later came to learn, was done by people who claim to have the inspiration of the Holy Spirit. If that be true, then from the bottom of my heart I do curse such 'Holy Spirit' powered brutes.

But that was a film shown by newsmen of the Uganda Television so it could have been acted, who knows - remember what the papers said: Some country up-north is getting film clips of the Amin days in order to scare and if possible rally the citizens against the impending invasion by a foreign army? Well maybe some official is in contact with an old German official who was in charge of filming during those Nazi days. Who knows, anything is possible in Uganda.

At any rate, I was not to be scared by the Uganda Television footage. With or without that film I was going to Gulu - home of my fore fathers to bathe in luxuriant Christmas weather. I got together my sisal basket and PIL plastic bag which contained a brand new silk gomesi which I had bought with my first salary for my dear mother; God bless her for having brought me into this sweet world. I then peered into a jagged mirror and saw a twenty-two-year-old teacher face. I smiled and it smiled; I gnashed and it gnashed and I knew that was me; Okema George, bachelor and teacher with two months experience. I gave a last look at my one-roomed house and whispered goodbye to it. As I latched the door and padlocked it with a Diamond padlock, I silently prayed that no 'good samaritan' should wish to help me sweep the accumulating dust for that is what they do in this section in Naguru Go down. The thieves are day-time thugs who, if caught, claim to be helping the owner to sweep the house clean - and in the process they really swept it clean, if you know what I mean. Anyway what can they steal from an already empty house? I consoled myself and with one nostalgic look, I turned my back to my house and made for the taxi-stage.

Kampala! Kampala! bayed the broker as if it was not obvious that the 'buffalo' taxi was directed towards Kampala. I rushed towards it because there was this gentleman who was making a beeline for the taxi which needed only one person before it could make its Kampala-bound journey. I shot my legs forward and before I knew it, my left leg which seemed in disagreement, had knocked a protruding rock and I was down flat passionately kissing the ground. The sisal bag flew off my grip and hit the baying broker, but by some luck the PIL plastic bag refused to obey the laws of physics and it remained in my grip. I got up and refused to hear what the broker was saying, after all it was in Luganda and I am one of those who obstinately refuse to learn any other Ugandan languages. So I kept mum, dusted myself, collected my scattered poverty and waited patiently for another taxi.

Now I am not the superstitious type, but as I looked at my sandaled left toe, a shiver went through me and I felt cold all over. I thought of going back to my room and leaving for Gulu after Christmas then I also thought of the smiling face of my mother and the adoration and honour that I would receive from the villagers and I made up my mind.

To hell with the superstitions! A taxi peep-peeped into my reverie. This time it was relatively empty so there was no need to rush but all the same, I was conscious as I walked. I got into the taxi and took a seat in the middle row. I am told that the first and last row are shock absorbers and with this pot-holed road of Naguru I was not taking any chances. The taxi was soon filled with Naguru dwellers and off we went to Kampala city. In ten minutes time we were at the Kampala taxi park. I paid the conductor three hundred shillings and began the walk towards Buganda bus park. I have always wondered why it is called so; I guess most buses are owned by the bourgeois Baganda. I was close to crossing the road when a mob of rough looking boys charged at me speaking in what I assumed was Luganda. I held my luggage tightly into my chest. Kampala was a dangerous city. Then I gave them an

Anyanya stare wide eyes, large nose and I weighed the rest of my force. They were taken aback. Then I heard.

'*I bi core* Gulu' Are you going to Gulu?

Talk about surprise. I was triple surprised - if such a surprise exists. Either the man who spoke those heart-pleasing words was also an *Anyanya* or he was an adopted Acholi. I replied in the affirmative and he pushed the other thugs aside and I felt like a presidential guest walking on a red carpet. We crossed the road - I still had my luggage on my chest - and he directed me to a Steyre bus. My hands quickly shot into my pocket and to my great relief my money was there. He then escorted me to the bus and just as I was about to enter the bus I felt a hand tapping my shoulder, I turned,

'How about my pay?' he asked in Acholi.

'What!' I was shocked.

'My money,' he said with a smile on his face. It's only then that I realised he had a gap between his teeth - the kind of gap you see when a door is opened.

'Do I owe you money?' I tried to be innocent.

'Yes, I helped you cross the road, I helped you find the bus to Gulu,' he replied confidently.

'How much?' I asked. I didn't want to be ungrateful.

'One thousand,' he stupidly flashed his gap.

'What! One thousand for just crossing the street and showing me the bus to Gulu?' I asked incredibly.

He nodded his head. I gave him my cold face, got onto the bus and got myself a seat. I was not going to be fooled. I have lived in Kampala long enough to know that silence is the best weapon.

Then I heard a shrill sound and looked out to see the group of thugs screaming and pointing at me from outside. The Samaritan turned devil was in the middle howling like a dog. I wondered what they were up to. Then I realised that they were drawing the attention of everyone around the bus. Those inside were looking at me as if I had ten ears.

If there is anything I hate, it is crowds; so I made a quick calculation. This man with a door gap between his teeth obviously wanted money and he was going to do anything to get it. I dropped my silence weapon and got out of the bus much to the relief of this door-gap man. He came round with his rowdy group with a triumphant look on their faces. I fished into my pocket and grudgingly gave him one thousand shillings. He then thanked me in Acholi. I was in no mood to answer. They then melted into the crowd and I got back into the bus where the occupants now looked at me as a fellow human being; a pair of eyes, two hands, two legs, two ears. Some even smiled at me. I got to my seat and sat. Uppermost in my mind was the thought that Isaac Newton should have thought out a fourth law of motion; where there is subtraction, there is addition; I was minus part of my hard earned money and the door-gap with his good for nothing imbeciles were one thousand shillings richer. Next time, I internally screamed to myself, 'I will not allow anyone to help me in a Kampala park-no-any park, be he a priest'. I even pinched myself and felt very good. I then closed my eyes, shifted my behind to get maximum comfort.

On opening my eyes, I decided to look around the bus which was quickly becoming an Acholi moving village. Most passengers were from the Acholi quarters of Kibuli - this I could tell by their apparent lack of dress harmony, mothers carrying babies on their backs and fronts, and the children who could walk had mucus oozing from their nostrils - then there were Acholis from the middle class - me inclusive - who were speaking in almost inaudible voices like they do in diplomatic circles. On the seats to the left of the driver were men who I could swear were not Acholis; they looked too exploitative to be Acholis, in fact they looked like businessmen. I guess they were going to Gulu to buy rice at two hundred shillings and sell it in Kampala at one thousand five hundred shillings. I think the term businessman is euphemism for parasite. There were two soldiers - I wondered where they were going and if they had their army pass books. One sat behind me and the other was next to the door. The rest of the passengers were the ordinary Gulu dwellers who sought to fleece a Kampala relative and were now taking the money home to squander it in K road and Alono night club.

Somebody must have tickled the driver who in turn tickled the passengers. He put into the bus cassette player an Afrigo Wa Wa tape and the loud speakers blared with *'O mama wange, mama wange.'* too loud I thought, but good. All the passengers reacted differently, those with babies rocked them to the rhythm of the song; the soldier next to the door fondled his gun as if it was the woman he danced with last night; when I turned to the one behind me he gave me a stony stare and I regretted having turned. The businessmen - sorry, parasites - simply nodded their heads in agreement with the bass voice of *wawa*. Those without dress harmony equally reacted without due respect to the tune - it was as if they were responding to a tune in their brains. And I? I reacted with a vigour and zest of a young Acholi, but unfortunately all that response was in my head hidden from all. You see teachers have to keep the ethical code of being an example - so I was being one.

The bus was like a moving disco hall with all passengers happy with the music save for the stony-eyed soldier behind me. Why had he sat behind me? - anyway we were all happy as the driver steered the Steyre through Kampala streets onto Bombo road on our way home. The further we were from Kampala, the louder the music and interestingly the passengers were silent. I tried to figure out what they were thinking; the businessmen must certainly be thinking of the huge profit they would get out of the ignorant Acholis; those who were from Kampala relatives must be contemplating on how to woo the fresh innocent and ignorant girls in Gulu and to brag to their less fortunate friends who do not have wealthy relatives in Kampala; those from Acholi quarters in Kibuli must be considering how to organise women in Pece in brewing *malwa* for higher profits; the soldier in front must certainly be thinking about the *Malaya* he had last night and the one behind me is undoubtedly thinking of items.

I stole a glance at him and - I couldn't believe it - he was sleeping, yes sleeping, and come to think of it everyone seemed to have thought themselves to sleep so who was I to watch over this Acholi humanity. I too thought myself to sleep.

I thought about the poverty-stricken noble profession that I serve; I thought about my beautiful girl - yes, I have one. In my mind, I saw my mother's face crack into a smile on seeing me and I saw her swoon in excitement on seeing the *gomesi*. I thought about a strange hand gently but insistently shaking me. I opened one eye and recognised the dirty shirt of the conductor and on opening the other eye, I saw the unshaven face and concluded that it was actually the conductor. 'What is it?' I dreamingly asked 'Road block ahead,' he replied and walked past my seat.

I sat up and sure enough, there was a road block ahead. Strange, I thought. A road block in the middle of nowhere I guess there were no houses within miles and the place was super empty anyway this is the way to the law and being a law abiding citizen I removed my identity card and waited. The rest of the passengers had been dutifully awakened by the conductor and they were fidgeting as they searched for their cards.

The bus came to a halt just before what looked like a large metal rod across the road and we all waited for there was no soul in sight. Five minutes, nothing happened. Ten minutes no one appeared. The passengers were beginning to get panicky. The soldiers were tightening their faces. Twenty minutes, nothing. The atmosphere was tense. The babies as if sensing danger, were silent as a rat hiding from an enraged cat. The women were looking to their husbands as if they were in control of the bus. The brave men did not dare to look out. The businessmen kept gazing at their briefcases that were next to them. I had an ice-cold feeling in my stomach. Twenty five minutes after we had stopped, it happened.

'Twa' a single shot broke through the driver's windscreen and his head slumped to one side in the posture of the dead. His blood was sprayed onto the female passenger behind him, who apparently had a phobia for human blood. She let out an ear-splitting scream that was taken up in choir fashion by the women in the bus - I don't know why women prefer screaming when in danger - and the whole bus became filled with their hysterical screams. Then I heard an earth shaking ka. Boom! '.... and I saw the door flung aside and those sitting opposite were the unfortunate human shield in the way of what I perceived was a rocket; They were forced out of the bus through its body into the open air, their flesh splattered all over the place.

Everything happened so fast. The women were screaming silently. The businessmen - when I looked in that direction - were as dead as death with their lifeless eyes staring into space. I will never know what happened to them. The soldier behind me, on seeing his dead colleague, foolishly rushed towards the door and met his death. What was out there did not like him. The bus began filling up with smoke and we were forced to find refuge outside. There was a stampede for the door. We all rushed out with our hands over our eyes and holding our noses to prevent the smoke from entering our eyes and the burning stench of human flesh from entering our lungs. When I had managed to get out, I slowly stopped squeezing my eyes and began to read my surrounding. Most of the passengers were out. Around us stood man-mountains; big, black dirty muscular men carrying rocket launchers and machine guns. It was then that I began racking my brains to find out what had happened to us. An ambush - yes - an ambush. The word rebels pounded in my brain and adrenalin triggered uncontrollable fear which in turn released my urinal tap - I hurriedly clutched my crotch but it was too late - urine flowed freely to my legs and the soil. I looked foolish, but this was not a time for diplomacy. We were doomed.

We were herded to about one hundred meters away then one of them knelt and fired at the wreck of the bus with a rocket launcher and we saw the bus going into flames with an ear-deafening sound. I visualized the burning flesh of the fatty businessmen and it was only then that I realised that my mother's gomesi had been left in the bus. Too bad. My eyes misted and I felt a few drops of tears on my cheeks.

'OK. Let's move!' One of those murderous fools barked in Kiswahili. And frightened as we all were, we obeyed and followed the thug in front.

Those behind, like me, had to be prodded with the butt of a gun to get the message. I guess everyone was so shocked at what had happened and as a result was silently contemplating the fate that had befallen them. As we grudgingly moved with those thugs moving menacingly by us, a woman in the middle stood still and began shaking all over as if she had an evil spirit in her - then she opened her mouth and let out a blood-curdling scream and began uttering; 'My child! My child! My child!' in increasing tempo. The reaction was automatic.

We all distanced ourselves from her as if she was emitting the deadly AIDS virus. From the corner of my eyes, I saw two huge thugs taking a step backwards. The rest of the thugs - they were about thirty were standing statue-like. The woman raked her hair and was foaming at the mouth, her eyes were in danger of exploding. Her shaking was now vigorous and no one dared to go close.

Suddenly she stopped. Her bulging eyes roved around and then slowly moved. Her eyes seemed to be searching, searching for something. She saw it. She began moving with outstretched arms.

Moving towards me. My God! I am dead!! My heart thumped and thumped! 'God please open the earth, let it swallow me' I pleaded and closed my eyes - I always close my eyes when afraid - and waited for the cold female finger on my neck. I felt a cold gust of wind go by me and I opened my eyes. She had run past me. Her target was the soldier behind me. She was screaming, 'You killed my child.'

She looked like a female puma about to tear apart its prey. The rebel stared at her not knowing what to do. Not knowing that he had a quick means to make this human nightmare disappear from the face of the earth. With the woman just five steps from him, the rebel soldier did the most militarily unthinkable thing, he closed his eyes and became stone-like. The woman took him by the neck and her hands were like a vice. She tightened her grip and I saw his trousers dampen and I realised the fellow was beyond help. I looked at the other hostages - in front of us with mouths agape. The other rebels were perplexed. Then I heard or rather smelt a nasty odour and it became clear that the rebel had defecated on himself.

The smell quickly enveloped us and it hit the rebels with a resounding blow. They quickly ran towards the woman with the limp rebel in her grip. She turned towards them and there was a red glow in her eyes. The rebels crouched and opened fire. The figure of the woman danced like a rag and fell heavily on the ground. One of those heartless fellows moved close and as if fearing that the woman might resurrect, he pointed his gun to the woman's head and pulled the trigger. The woman's head was within seconds turned into a neat pile of minced meat. He then nodded satisfactorily and turned to us with a gaze that challenged any of us to do what the pile of human flesh next to him had done and for good measure he ordered that the youngest person be brought forth.

The soldiers obeyed. A girl of about twelve years was grabbed and frog-marched to the rebel from whom the order had ensued.

'Lie down,' he ordered.

The innocent looking girl was afraid. She knew she was going to die so she did the next most logical thing, she tried to resist,

Please don't kill me,' she pleaded.

'Shut up and obey the commander!' the rebels from behind her shouted.

So this fellow was the commander. We were quickly herded into a semi-circle from where the stench of human flesh was becoming unbearable.

I felt for this girl but I was not going to change places.

Her pleas were cut short by a stinging panga slap that landed squarely onto her cheek. She fell just before the shoes of the commander who promptly put his heavy shoes onto her neck. I could hear her trying to scream but the heartless one made sure she did not have enough mouth space to scream. He then asked for a panga which was given. He then made the sign of the cross and all the other rebels knelt and he did the same. I was as confused as the other hostages. Then he looked directly into the sun and seemed to draw his strength from it. His eyes became so wide, I thought they would pop out. His breathing became heavy; you could hear it miles away. Then the rebels around us let out a hyena kind of laugh that started at a low pitch and increased in tempo. When it had reached climax, the commander did it. Yes, he did it. He raised the panga high above his head and bought it down on the back of the girl and believe it - the body was halved into two. Then he quickly proceeded to hew the limbs as he was screaming. When his job was done he lifted the panga to his tongue and licked it. He then looked at us with a triumphant look and smiled. I looked at the other hostages and they all looked like they had seen death.

We had all witnessed a ritual - a terrible one - and somehow we were all guilty of not doing anything - but what does one do against such murderous heartless beasts.

19
A Hospital on the Kampala-Gulu Road
Dr Stanley Kiwanuka Kitaka

On 27th January 1986, disaster struck my place of work; Kiryandongo Hospital in Masindi District. I was working as a Medical Superintendent of that hundred-bed government hospital situated 130 miles on Kampala-Gulu Road. I was the only doctor among a staff of 150 employees.

The government in Kampala, headed by General Tito Okello Lutwa, had fallen to the victorious National Resistance Army (NRA) led by Yoweri Museveni. Defeated soldiers from Kampala mainly took the Kampala-Gulu road on their way to the North. They committed atrocities as they retreated; mainly in the form of killing innocent civilians, looting property, raping and setting people's houses on fire. They had special hatred against people coming from the South and West of Uganda because these formed the bulk of the NRA.

Hundreds and hundreds of these soldiers had arrived overnight and camped at Kiryandongo trading centre with the hope of commandeering lorries and other vehicles to proceed to Gulu and other places. Throughout the night of 26th January 1986 they were banging people's houses, looting shops and also firing aimlessly.

At about 6.30 a.m, four of these soldiers forced their way into my house via the hind door. They immediately put me and the family members at gun-point. They were of dark complexion and appeared to be of Nubian extraction from Southern Sudan. They were in mid-twenties and spoke Swahili. They were armed with AK 47s and hand grenades. They hurriedly asked for money, radio cassettes and watches. I gave them the money I had (I do not remember the exact amount) and they left with my radio cassette and my Oris watch. None of the family members was hurt.

My wife Eva, who was six months pregnant, was extremely terrified. During that brief ordeal, she was in tears and pleading with the soldiers not to harm me. The housegirl Night was equally terrified while my son Paul Kiwanuka was still asleep.

Fearing that soon another group of soldiers might come and demand money and other valuables, we decided to run away from the hospital at about 8.30 a.m. We carried a few personal items and left via the cemetery path. We did not have any particular destination to head to.

On our way to nowhere, we were joined by other hospital staff and villagers. We travelled for about 4km and camped at Mr. Kasigwa's residence at a place called Kijuna. This was relatively free from the terror of the retreating soldiers. By coincidence, Mr. Kasigwa was the Hospital's water pump mechanic. He welcomed us warmly and gave me a room in the boys' quarters.

We stayed at this man's place for three days while at the same time monitoring the situation at the hospital and the trading centre. All sorts of rumours were circulating concerning the whereabouts of the NRA.

A day following our departure from the hospital, sad news came to the effect that a Medical Assistant by the name of Ago had been shot dead in the hospital compound.

Furthermore, that all hospital quarters (Senior & Junior) had been thoroughly looted by the retreating soldiers. Meanwhile, daytime was boring with hardly anything to do. I patiently kept a low profile because I did not want people to know my hideout. The nights were more terrifying with sporadic gunfire and explosions being heard in the direction of the hospital and trading centre. Soldiers were on a rampage, breaking into abandoned houses.

On the third day after escaping from the hospital, news came that the NRA was advancing towards Kiryandongo and we were instructed to move deeper into the villages. We shifted and headed for a forest some 5 km from Kasigwa's residence. This new station was called Nyakarongo.

We stayed in the open for two memorable days feeding on cassava and potatoes provided by the locals. After two days' stay at Nyakarongo, news came that Kiryandongo had been liberated and we were free to return to our residences. We breathed with relief.

The next day we returned to the hospital only to find misery. All our houses had been broken into and swept clean. Every movable item had gone! Doors were ajar, windows smashed, torn papers were everywhere. The few items that we had run away with became the most valuable property in our possession.

Deep in my mind, I cursed war and all it stood for. It had reduced us to destitutes in just a matter of days! However, consolation came from the fact that we were still alive and we had been liberated by people with a vision.

As for the hospital, it looked more like a military barracks than a treatment centre. Hundreds and hundreds of NRA soldiers including the famous Kadogos were everywhere. Very few of them had army uniform, the majority were in tattered civilian attire. They were in high spirits having dealt the enemy a decisive blow so far. Some were cooking, others fetching water and also combing the area for any remnants of the enemy. They all looked friendly and welcoming. In addition, there were many Army trucks with mounted heavy guns all pointing in the direction of Karuma. Among these soldiers were females, some with high ranks. Not far from the entrance to the main hospital complex, there was a huge gathering surrounding four captured enemy soldiers. They had been tied *Kandoya* or 'three piece' as it was called and they were pleading for mercy from their interrogators. I had never seen that way of tying people.

As head of the hospital I held discussions with one of the NRA Battalion leaders by the name of Commander Dr. Mugambwa. He was not strange to me because we had met in the medical school some years back as students. He was two years ahead of me. He informed me that the units were heading for Karuma bridge and that the hospital was going to act as their medical base for the time being. In addition, he assured me that the staff were going to be assisted with some of their rations. As for security there was nothing to fear or worry about. Furthermore he said that unlike the defeated soldiers, the NRA was a disciplined force with a proper chain of command and respect for the civilians. Though drugs and sundries stores had been thoroughly looted, the main theatre was still in working condition. We prepared to receive casualties from the warfront ahead.

As for the staff, morale was extremely low because of the extensive looting of their personal belongings. Most of their houses were lacking doors and window panes. There was no water or electricity. Worse still there was no transport or communication. The only hospital ambulance, a Land Rover, had already been sent to the front line at Karuma by the NRA.

A day following our return, casualties started arriving from the front line at Karuma.

I and Dr Mugambwa operated throughout the night. One of those badly injured soldiers had been shot in the abdomen and was brought in around midnight in a shocked state. Under intensive resuscitation a laporotomy was done to repair his stomach and small gut. Due to lack of blood he passed away soon after the operation. May his soul rest in eternal peace. The battle for Karuma was heavy and the casualties were many. After two weeks, the NRA medical team left the hospital and moved northwards with the advancing mobile brigades.

Thereafter members of the International Committee of the Red Cross visited the hospital and they offered relief items to the staff and the local community. They also supplied some drugs and sundries. This was a big morale booster.

Administratively I moved to link up with the DMO'S office in Masindi as well as the Ministry of Health Headquarters in Entebbe. Gradually, the hospital started offering limited services to the people and at the same time, life returned to normal. A new chapter had been opened in our area as well as in the whole motherland of Uganda.

20
A West Nile Bandit in the City
Yuni Mí

It all started with a story entitled 'Tragedy in East Moyo' on 11th March 1981 in *Uganda Times*, the then leading government mouthpiece. The story headline stood out in clear block capitals to tell every Ugandan that 'something' was up, and East Moyo was no more or, as the story said, 'Humbled to its knee'.

I was working in an industry in Jinja but I come from East Moyo Adjumani, to be precise. As I read the story over and over again, I became more and more anxious. It described my exact home area, the spot where I was born and grew up. I could picture every little item in the location.

When I got home I tried to hide the story from my family. So I went straight to my bedroom and dumped the paper in a cupboard. My wife, who knew my moods well enough, realised something was wrong and followed me to find out. By the time she got to the bedroom door, I was already closing it and only told her I was going out.

I hoped to meet my kinsmen at a drinking place, where we usually converged to pass evenings, to console myself. Most of them had read the paper and so the atmosphere at the pub was tense. Nobody could console another. We emptied bottles over bottles of beer and got hopelessly drunk that evening without getting any better words or news about East Moyo than the paper had reported.

When I got back home from the bar, I tossed in bed without much sleep. At dawn, an idea came to me that there was a better place to gather information from in Kampala than the bar I went to. This was an old building just opposite the Bank of Uganda, which got burnt immediately after the UNLF took over power. This place was nicknamed 'Achifu', meaning ashes. It was the main unofficial meeting place for the majority of people from West Nile region to gather information about what was going on in the region.

Early in the morning I went to work and created a good reason for my boss to release some money for me to go to Kampala to find out more about the story that appeared in the papers. Indeed, in truth, my boss saw the sense in settling my anxiety.

By 10:00 am, I was already in Kampala and went straight to Achifu. There were cross-sections of people in the place. The first to catch my sight was an old schoolmate who quickly welcomed me with a glass of *lira-lira*. When I had sipped a good part of the *enguli* my friend told me he had just come from the Kivukoni School of political ideology in Tanzania. He was employed with the National Security Agency (NASA). They moved freely to more parts of the country in the company of ministers, members of parliament and some high ranking government and military officers.

This story did not interest me much but I listened on since I hoped he would be a good source of information to satisfy my curiosity. At long last, he pulled out the newspapers from his briefcase and pointed at the headline 'Tragedy in East Moyo' and sadly said 'see this story l have just come back from Adjumani in company of Ben Bella, the Editor of Uganda Times, Tito Okello , Moses Apiliga and some of my colleagues to assess this tragedy.'

My eyes beamed. I had come to the root of what I wanted but l did not interrupt him. I just listened on. The man in his sad note continued to tell me that he visited my home area. 'There are no houses standing. 'NO single house and no people there.' 'Terrible, I saw only a few people gathered at the mission. It was misery.' The man stared into the air and shook his head, suddenly he burst out again. 'Yes your mother was in the crowd of the mission. I did not see any of your brothers and sisters there. Sorry, I do not know their fate. But keep calm. My group will go back in a week's time and I shall keep you posted.'

When he finished his story, I was sure the tragedy involved my close relatives. My houses at home were destroyed and most likely, I had lost some people as well. The man was concealing some information from me. The anxiety of the previous evening returned with more certainty. I continued to gulp more *enguli*.

By the time I realised I should go back to Jinja it was late. I went to the taxi park but I could not get a taxi to Jinja because at that time vehicles going out of Kampala had stopped, leave alone those moving within Kampala itself, for fear of harassment by soldiers at the road blocks.

Since no vehicles could take me to Jinja I had to spend the night in Kampala. So I walked back to Achifu but my friend had gone. There was no other person I knew well in the area. Everyone was leaving the place which now looked dirtier than before. I stood at the door for a moment wondering and my mind went to a friend I knew some years back when I was still an undergraduate student at Makerere. This friend stayed in Naguru housing estate. I knew he would accommodate me for a night at this time of crisis. So I set off for Naguru on foot, sure to get there before sunset. To my surprise when I reached Lugogo indoor stadium, I found a number of people who were heading to Naguru, Nakawa, Bugolobi, Kyambogo and Banda, but stopped by the soldiers. Just opposite the Lugogo indoor stadium there was a garage for Military hardware. It was the soldiers guarding the garage who stopped these people.

One of the soldiers was tall and dark skinned with knock knees and another one was short and light skinned. The two soldiers ordered us to move to the garage. On reaching the garage, the tall soldier interviewed us in Luo while the short one did so in Luganda. Those who passed the language test were released. I failed this test and that was my crime number one.

When those who were successful in the first test left, the tall soldier turned to me and asked in a poor accent Kiswahili *'wewe ona toka wapi?'* I told him I came from Jinja. That was a misfire because I did not know Luganda/ Lusoga. So he asked me again *'Watu ya Jinja ona jua Kiganda kuna nini wewe a pana jua'*. I told him I worked in Jinja but I was not born there.

'Tena wewe ona zaliwa wapi?' I answered I was from West Nile . That name of West Nile was the second crime because West Nile was connected with dictator Idi Amin so the man became more furious.

'Wewe ni kabila gani?' I told him I was Madi. This was crime number three.

'Wewe ni Madi ya wapi.' I was in trouble. I could read death in the man's eyes. So instinctively I told him I came from Adjumani. This was my fourth crime which was a capital offence because Adjumani was a wrong spot at that time when and where the tragedy had occurred.

These crimes were magnified fourfold. The soldiers claimed that Adjumani incident was sparked off by a bandit who shot a military vehicle. After the Adjumani incident, another group of bandits attacked a military unit at Rhino camp and killed UNLA soldiers, including a captain.

Therefore according to this soldier, a man from West Nile region who could speak neither Luo nor Luganda was automatically a bandit, a Madi was a real bandit, and that from Adjumani where a series of incidences had occurred was probably the cause of these incidences and the one who killed the captain at Rhino camp. So, by this intuitive judgement I was labelled, judged and condemned a first class criminal/bandit who must be killed on sight.

The knock-kneed soldier sweated in anger as he talked while his counterpart, the short one, gently got hold of and scrutinised all my documents. He then took my bag, emptied its contents and inspected them one by one to satisfy himself that I was a civil servant who had lived and paid taxes outside the West Nile region for more than ten years, despite my origin from Adjumani. So on the one hand I was a clean citizen, a simple humble civil servant as judged by my documents, while on the other hand I was a first class bandit /criminal as judged by my ethnic origin.

Then there was division in the military camp about my fate when the short soldier talked with all the calmness and sympathy possible that he found nothing wrong with my documents to convict me so his colleague could let me go free. This enraged the tall soldier who instantly demanded to see my documents himself. However, before he was given the documents he murmured some words I could not follow; moved a few steps backwards and cocked his gun; his counterpart dived in time to grab the gun before it could crack. The tall man violently ordered his colleague to give back his gun, which he did, but before doing so the short soldier was smart enough to remove the magazine from the gun. This annoyed the man even more because his gun could not shoot. He ordered me to leave immediately. I bent down to pick my bag but the man shouted at me to leave it. He jumped and gave me a heavy kick with the military boot. I gave him the bag and moved a few steps away from the man. He got the gun by the barrel and swung the butt furiously to hit my head as I moved. I dived down so he missed me smartly. The heavy swing sent him in heavy trouble on the ground. He murmured a few curses against me as he struggled to get up.

This was my fifth crime that evening, to have dodged a soldier's beating. The man got up with all the anger and grabbed me. Before his sympathetic colleague could rush to my rescue he had beaten me three or four times with the butt of the gun and was breathing heavily in satisfaction. I could not remember which blow sent me down but I was lying helpless. The brown soldier held his counterpart to prevent him from giving me any more beating and told me to move away.

As I moved from the scene of the scuffle it was almost dark. I reached the house I was going to in Naguru when it was dark and my friend was not there. The house had been taken over by an old man who spoke to me in Luo. My heart leaped into my throat. I felt as good as dead. I told him my friend's name and he agreed to show me where he had shifted to. I mistrusted his promise for I associated Luo with more danger, more beating and probably death. He saw my reluctance but assured me that my friend lived only a few meters away.

When we reached the house my friend welcomed me. I told him the story. He was amused. That was the order of events in Kampala then, rampant gunshots he called 'pop corns' was the normal music every night. Soldiers looted civilians as they wished and I was a victim of this order of events.

I did not satisfy my curiosity to find out more about the tragedy in East Moyo, instead I became a bandit in the city and was almost killed. I went back to Jinja more disappointed then I came.

21
The Dumping Grounds
Joshua Kato

Like many people in the city, Ben (as friends and relatives loved to call him) was born in Luwero district. He was actually one of the eldest sons of Mzee Eriferitisa Kasolo, a large estates farmer at Nakaseke.

In his teens, Ben left Nakaseke for Kampala in order to receive quality education from Kampala schools. Very soon, he completed his 'A' level at Kampala Secondary School with flying colours which earned him a scholarship to study in England. When he came back in the late 1960s he opened up a flour mill in Kawempe, while at the same time working as a food chemist at the then giant Mukisa biscuits. With a happy family and a big salary he was certainly set for greater heights.

At the time of his capture in December 1982, he was 48 years old and a proud owner of a Mercedes Benz automobile and a Peugeot 204 box body that he mainly used to carry materials for his flour mill. Then things changed suddenly.

As NRA guerrillas intensified their attacks in Luwero, rumours of infiltration into the city by some of their commandos became rife. The government security organisations moved to tame the situation. However, the system was brutally abused by the rank and file in the various security organisations, namely NASA (National Security Agency), GSU (General Safety Unity) and Special Force. Many people were erroneously 'sectioned' as being rebels, they were arrested, and very few of them left the torture chambers alive. Incidentally, personal grudges ranging from being wealthier than a NASA boss, or falling in love with the same woman as a NASA, GSU or special force man played a greater role than being a real rebel collaborator. Such was the case with Ben.

Time check, 10:00 mid morning: Tuesday 1st December 1982.

Two things happened almost at the same time in Ben's Flour mill. One of the ropes on one of the machines snapped, and then a red Peugeot 504 pulled up just next to the door. Even before it stopped, two stout men donning dark goggles jumped out, followed by the third who was also the driver. In the blink of an eye, they took positions on either side of the door, before entering with their black pistols at the ready. The story is recounted by Musisi, then a casual labourer in the mill.

Ben was a tough man so he could not be easily cowed. A fierce confrontation broke out between him and the three stout NASA men. However, after about five minutes of serious fist and kick fights, they overpowered him and then dumped him in the boot of their Peugeot. Before they went away, they fired several shots in the mill machines, wrecking them.

* * *

At home in Kisaasi, Mrs. Kasolo, her young children and Ben's elderly mother Catherine Kasolo had just finished having lunch when Musisi rushed in with the news.

'He has been arrested by men who said they were policemen, we don't know where he was taken, they sped away like a rally car', he explained pantingly.

Mrs. Kasolo quickly dressed up and rushed to Kawempe in order to confirm the news. Several questions had to be asked, but answering them was another problem. Where could they begin the search for Ben?

'Fear was rife,' Musisi explains, 'That is when someone was arrested in such a manner, even those people seeking to find where he has been kept were sometimes arrested, that was the first hurdle to cross.'

Before the day ended, Mrs. Kasoslo, escorted by Senkunda, who was Ben's eldest son, had visited basically all police stations in the city to seek any information that night have led to the discovery of Ben, but all had come to naught.

After three days of a traumatic and uncertain wait, a family friend who had earlier discovered her husband's body in Namanve forest paid the family a visit. She was of the view that perhaps they try all avenues of finding Ben whether alive or dead, including going and looking at the dead bodies in Namanve forest and then Busabala, another dumping ground near the lake. Obviously, however painful the decision was, none of the family members objected. With the killings then, anything was possible.

The next day, Mrs. Kasolo and Ben's elder son Senkunda woke up very early and braced themselves for perhaps the most fearful and traumatic mission of their lives. But even then, they were expecting to find the body, but also praying that he was not dead, but safe somewhere and would be back before they came back.

Nonetheless, they boarded a Mukono-bound taxi which dropped them in the middle of the forest as directed by the family friend. Even on the road the place had an eerie deathly atmosphere. Winds splashing through the leaves of the tall trees made it even more eerie, perhaps a place somewhere in hell. Vehicles on the main Jinja road were occasional, and very speedy, thus insignificant.

Senkunda takes up the story

We began following a small path down the forest as directed by the family friend. We did not need to go far because about 100 metres down the forest our noses brought it all. And then almost immediately we bumped into the first body! It was a mangled piece of human flesh, perhaps a day old in the forest. But even then, hundreds of the huge blue flies had already swarmed over it, giving it a more weird look.

'I was the most courageous and so I picked up a tree branch and swung it over the flies. They flew, but only for a moment because they soon settled back,' Senkunda said. 'But by the time they settled back, we had already examined the head and confirmed that it was not Ben's. The power of the foul smell emanating from the rotting bodies nauseated our souls, but even then, we had been told right from childhood that vomiting or spitting because of smell coming from dead human bodies was a taboo. We held our breath.

About 50 meters down the path, we bumped into more bodies. This time they were strewn almost as far as the eye could see, sprawled in all forms in spaces between the trees on an area of over 200 meters. Humanity had lost meaning, it had become cheaper than salt, so cheap to maintain, so cheap to guard.

Back to the bodies, it was a mixture of every kind of man. Most of them were naked apart from their underpants. Some were flesh, others had began decomposing while the majority had turned into skeletons.

Meanwhile, prey-eating birds, especially marobou storks, were having a field day, pulling away at flesh at will. They were perhaps celebrating! We soon made certain that Ben was not among the dead and so we moved out of the forest, traumatised to the maximum.

We boarded a taxi to the city, before boarding another one to the lakeside village of Busabala where another dumping ground was. As soon as we reached there, we came across two young men just on the edge of the forest. 'Looking for a relative?' one of them asked.

'Yes, he was arrested a week ago, we suspect he is now dead', Senkundo answered.

'Follow that path, into the valley, there were a fresh dumping last night, your relative might be one of them,' the boy said. They further explained that both of them were casual labourers who carried dead bodies from the valley for a few shillings. Before we began walking down the path, two other families joined us, giving us confidence that we were not alone.

The smell of rotting flesh hit us from afar; thus, we used our hankies to shield our noses from the dangerously nauseating smell. Very soon, we bumped into the first heap of bodies which from a distance looked like a huge heap of blueflies, on trees. Flesh eating vultures and storks had already had a field day because their food storage parts were full but perhaps they were waiting for another uninterrupted chance to feast again.

The bodies themselves were 19 in number, some half-dressed but the majority completely naked. They had been dumped in a heap obviously the night before. However, even then those on top had already lost their eyes to the vultures. The ever present blueflies had already laid their eggs in the empty eye sockets. One by one, we examined the bodies in the first heap, but none was Ben's. However one of the other two families found their dead relative who was stark naked, without eyes and missing his left arm. Soon, the two young men were paid Shs.5,000/- for carrying the body up the hill onto a waiting pick-up.

Although they had carried away a dead body, we envied them because they had been more successful than we had. On the other hand, their success gave us more vigour to look for Ben. We moved on to the second heap, which was perhaps a week old in the forest. These were 15 bodies all men, their skins had began peeling off and most of them were in their primary levels of decomposition. Nonetheless, they were still identifiable. None of them was Ben's. Down the depths of the forest, the rest of the bodies were no longer identifiable, all were decomposed almost to skeleton level. Humanity had lost meaning.

With our heads bowed and energy gone, with our souls dampened by the dangerous smell, with our minds traumatised because of what we had seen, we moved out of the forest. A human abattoir to be precise, a human garbage dumping ground to be realistic.

* * *

For the next six days, they paid daily visits to the dumping grounds but never discovered Ben. Then on the 14th day of his arrest Arnold Byamugisha, a well known NASA boss, paid the family a visit. Like any sympathetic family friend, he promised to help look for his friend Ben.

'Yes, I will help, but those people need money. Perhaps if you can raise 0.6 million as quick as possible, I might find him as early as next week,' Byamugisha told them. Unaware that this NASA man was the cause of Ben's disappearance, most family members clapped and warmly thanked him.

Raising the money was another problem. But on the next day, Senkunda (Ben's elder son) left for Bululi in Luwero district where most of Ben's relatives had taken refuge, on the second of Mzee Kasolo's several estates. Going out of Kampala, especially to Luwero was not easy, but coming back was even worse because of the so many harsh road blocks on the way. Killing people at the road blocks was the soldiers' speciality and depriving them of their valuables was a major tactic.

Such conditions put into consideration, the family members in Bululi, after selling four cows and raising the required amount, tailored two secret pockets inside Senkunda's underwear where they hid the money. The next day Senkunda successfully brought it to Kampala, where it was immediately handed to Byamugisha.

'I am going to try even today' he said with a giant cheek to cheek grin covering his wide face. He promised to bring back some good news on that day. He left the Kasolo's in anticipation.

In the evening, Byamugisha came back but he only excused himself saying that he had been busy for the whole day. He however promised to be more serious on the next day which was a Saturday. Indeed, no one doubted what he said mainly because of the undistorted concern that appeared on his face whenever he talked about Ben.

On Saturday, more tragedy struck as news came through from Nakaseke that one of Ben's young brothers Kaweesa had been killed by government troops on suspicion of being a rebel sympathiser. Meanwhile, Byamugisha brought back some news.

I have managed to locate Ben in a secret cell at Makindye military barracks, but not before dishing out all the money to unscrupulous army captains. I need another 0.4 million shillings before the captains allow you to see him, Byamugisha told the family.

There were mixed reactions by the family to Byamugisha's statements, this was mainly because, although they were happy on learning that their loved one was alive and kicking, there was a serious hurdle of finding the 0.4 million shillings.

Incidentally, going back to Bululi was out of question because in the last two days, reports had come through that NRA guerrillas had cut off the main Kampala-Gulu road just after Luwero town. Thus, the only option around was to look around in the city. After a consensus, three cows were sold and the money raised. Soon it was delivered to Byamugisha. Like on the previous occasion, he grinned widely, tucked the money in his brief case before he promised to do something quickly.

Four days later, he suddenly told them in the evening that they will be visiting Ben the next day with him at Makindye. Every family member waited in anticipation. Early the next morning, they were driven by Byamugisha in a UC registered Land Rover V8 to Makindye.

Senkunda takes up the story

I and Mrs. Kasolo went. In our possession was some well-cooked food, some clothes and water. All the way to Makindye, Byamugisha involved us in all kinds of discussions, including talking about the brutality of some of the troops. But soon we arrived at Makindye. After being thoroughly searched at the quarter guard, we were led into a small room where Byamugisha left us.

After some time, he came back with an army captain. 'How are you?' he greeted us.

'Alright' we answered shakily. It was obvious from the way he spoke that he already knew why we had gone there.

'I am captain Okello Paul,' he said. 'Ben is in a cell in this barracks but it is not possible to see him today.' He paused, 'The charges against him are tough, so go back home and bring 0.6 million shillings and that is when you will be allowed to see him.'

'What are the charges?' I asked.

The question angered the Captain. 'That is none of your business, do you want to interfere with army work? Eeh? Go and do as I have said or else he will die!' Okello boomed out loudly.

Shaking and bewildered by the sudden change of events, we walked out of the barracks with mixed feelings. At the quarter guard, two soldiers who checked us out did not hesitate to grab the food we had brought for Ben. As we walked away, I took a glance back at the sprawling barracks, the men at the quarter guard, the soldiers and, yes, that captain who within me I thought could not save my father.

We went back home and once again pondered where we could get the money to see Ben. The only viable options we had were selling the cars, mainly the Peugeot 204. Worse still, finding a buyer turned out to be another problem. Many businessmen in Kawempe who were approached to buy the car refused as soon as they realised that the owner was in prison. After over a week of searching, one Musoke, a businessman in Bwaise offered a paltry 1.5 million for the car. Nonetheless, we accepted because it was an emergency.

Exactly 40 days after he was arrested, I and Mrs Kasolo (my Mummy) saw him for the first time. As soon as we delivered the money to captain Okello's office, he directed us to the same small room and in five minutes he appeared with Ben before us.

There he is, he is in sound mind, though he is complaining of some illness, but he is not seriously ill, the captain told us.

Everyone was dumbfounded. If we had a right, we would have denied the slim looking man straight away! Ben normally kept a beard but this was more than we had bargained for, it was a forest on his face! He was barely dressed with his countable ribs visible through what was once a shirt. His whole body was bruised with an ugly wound prominently featuring on his face. It was terrible.

'Can't you people talk? Eeh?' captain burst out, 'Are you not happy finding him alive ? You have got only fifteen minutes to talk and to leave this place. Do it now!'

Instead of greetings, tears began dropping freely on all our faces, we were lost for words.

Then Ben broke the silence. 'How are you, my children and relatives. How is my father, how is everyone?' he asked, revealing an almost rotten mouth and teeth.

'Everything would have been OK if you are not here, maybe it will be OK when you leave but now it's not OK,' Mummy replied tearfully. After a pause she asked again, 'When will you be released?'

'I don't know, I can't say, I can't predict,' Ben replied.

He ate the food as quickly as possible, changed his clothes under the eyes of the captain. Then, like in the previous situation, all of a sudden, captain turned angrily, he suddenly walked forward, pulled Ben by the hip and dragged him away. He only managed a little bye-bye before he disappeared. We were all left tearfully.

Two days later, we went back to Makindye, introduced ourselves to the captain's office before he directed us to the same waiting room. However, it was obvious in the way we talked and felt inside that something was wrong. What came next confirmed our fears.

Even before we settled, a heavily armed soldier burst into the room, gave us a chit from captain and ordered us to leave immediately. It read: 'I am sorry, but your criminal husband was killed last night by our loyal forces as he tried to escape from prison. I am afraid you will never see his body again –' After an unexplained dash, it continued: 'Leave this place and never come back again.'

Even before we digested the message in the chit, the soldier cocked his gun and ordered us to leave. We scrambled out with tears flowing freely from our eyes!

The next week was even more traumatic than the last 40 days. This is because though we had confirmed that Ben was dead, we did not know where his body was. As a result, we moved from dumping ground to dumping ground but that did not yield any results. Two weeks later, we finally painfully accepted the new situation, but continued praying that one day Ben's remains will be found and given a decent burial. That has never happened.

Ben is still remembered by his children Senkunda Mefiasi, Kangave Livingstone, Muwanga David, Kibuuka Benjamin, Kasolo Erias, Lusoose and Zawedde.

May his soul rest in peace.

22
An Encounter with Friendly Enemies
Fortunate Tabaro Nkera

Each time I look back at those days I spend several minutes, sometimes hours, asking myself where we Ugandans would be if things had kept at that footing. This was the Obote II era in the 1980s. During that time I was a Senior Secondary student at St. Paul's Mutolere Secondary School, Kisoro district.

To us, the sons of the lower cadre civil servants, and our brethren, the sons of peasants, life was always a bed of thorns. We never had an extra shilling to buy ourselves a plate of hastily boiled beans and potatoes to supplement the miserable and half cooked shares served in the dining hall. Two tablets of soap usually took us through the term. The meaning of this was that in a term of three months, bathing was done thrice, only about six times would one wash his school uniform; and only once would we wash our bed sheets and the rest of the clothes – in most cases two threadbare shirts and two faded pairs of trousers. Told about our feet, the student of today would burst his/her ribs with peals of laughter. Most students had only one old pair of shoes, and a pair of slippers, rich with copper wire, nylon strings and bits of leather which held it together precariously. Personally during my O-Level, I owned only one pair of slippers whose straps later protested, and broke as my feet unfortunately swelled bigger and bigger with age, before I could see the end of my course. Thereafter, I started dragging my bare feet all around the school compound, and occasionally I would hide them in the old pair of shoes once belonging to my father which I had one day discovered in a musty box somewhere in our house.

One holiday, during those difficult days, a friend of mine; also a classmate, and a poverty-mate too, came to my father's house late in the evening. His face was all smiles and he breathed hard, evidently with urgent news, and presumably good news. His name was Kapachare. Before we had even greeted each other, Kapachare was already telling me how he had landed on spotlessly clean money, inviting me to come and share the money. If I let the money flow into other hands, Kapachare said, I would be no less stupid than the foolish dog which lay watching while its kin and kith enjoyed the occasion of a cow's death.

The source of the money was as simple as the boy himself: Hanja, a successful farmer in our village, had got a sack of beans and two cartons of hoes that he wanted to smuggle across the boarder into Rwanda. But as everyone knew, Hanja could not hire anybody's car to transport the goods. They would end up in the hands of policemen at the road blocks along the Kabale-Katura road. And that is why Kapachare had come to see me. Already he had secured two boys, Kakomo and Rwamutare, to carry the hoes while he and I would share the beans, each of us carrying a bag of fifty kilograms. Once we had returned bearing handsome bob, Hanja would surely reward us beautifully. Kapachare had merely pushed to the ground an already squatting man, for who was I to reject such money? I started planning how I would buy myself new clothes, and how I would not starve again once the school had opened.

'Kapachare,' I found myself screaming with jollity, 'When we appear at school next term, we shall be completely metamorphosised!' 'OK, keep quiet about it.' Kapachare was too pleased to talk more.

The following evening, as dusk crept in, Kapachare and I were already at Hanja's house. We were sitting at a bench on the verandah. Hanja had already filled the beans in two 50 Kg bags, which together with the cartons of hoes lay on the floor in the ante-room of the farmer's house.

Shortly after the two boys had come, Maria, Hanja's wife, brought in a Katogo of peas, Irish potatoes and pumpkins. We washed our hands and crammed our tummies, eating even the crumbs that accidentally dropped on the table for who knew whether we would get lunch, leave alone breakfast, the next day?

After the meal, we balanced the sacks and cartons on our heads, and departed. The murky blanket of night had descended on every home, everyone, and everything.

As we moved up a hill, sagging under the bulky sacks and cartons, rivulets of sweat rolling down our temples, foreheads and necks, I dug my right toe into a dwarf tree stump, and reeled forward and backward, but never fell. How soon man adapts to the odd life that necessity brings his way!

Descent followed ascent, and the journey wore on. We had crossed three separate swamps and four separate streams. Each one of us was breathing like bull.

'Are we now near the border?' I whispered, asking Kapachare. He was in front of me. The other two boys were behind me.

'Yes,' he said, 'As near to the border as the sun is near to the earth.'

I felt all the sweat dry off my body instantly. What was I to do? Already I felt like stopping and have a rest. Twice, I had caught myself dozing off with all the 50 Kg on my head. Jesus! I thought of allowing everyone to pass me, after which I would abandon my sack and hurry back home. But would I not lose my way? And if I did not lose it, would Hanja not castrate me? I bore my cross and travelled on.

After a long ordeal, I heard the first cock-crow. Near by, two or three birds started to twitter. We were now descending a very steep hill.

'At the foot of this hill, we shall cross a swamp which marks the boarder between Uganda and Rwanda,' I heard Kakomo telling Rwamutwe.

The eastern horizon was getting golden and darkness slowly gave way to a dense milky fog. Hill tops were now vaguely discernible, and silhouettes of trees and shrubs punctuated the whole hill slope. I could not have been more happy. The terrible dark night was finally wearing away.

We had just walked into the swamp when we hard a loud volley: Boom! It scattered us into disarray, leaving our beans and hoes in the swamp. Just as we started running a hoarse voice broke out like a rusty can: Stop where you are. You are surrounded! I stopped. I presume my pals also stopped. All of you come here, or a bullet. The voice ended its message half way through, but nothing could have been clearer.

My feet drove me towards the voice, and as I moved I almost bumped into someone. I jolted backward. It was a soldier holding his gun at the ready. Very soon, my three friends appeared at the scene. Soon after, another person materialised out of the dark shrubs, another soldier.

We were now shivering out of cold, mingled with fear, when our consolation came: 'Young fellows,' the second soldier said, 'We mean no harm to you. Otherwise we should have annihilated you, for you came when we were clearly seeing you! You see. Personally I have no grudge with citizens who make their ends meet. So boys, get your *magendo*, and have your luck!'

Before the word luck was out of the soldier's mouth, we had fallen on our luggage, raising it up on our heads.

The first soldier checked our haste: 'Caution boys. You are going to sell your coffee or whatever you are carrying and return home. But I am saying caution. Soldiers are stationed at several points along the border. And you never know.'

'They may not be as human, as parental as ourselves. They may molest you, take your money and imprison you. So to avoid any calamities, pass through this selfsame route on your way home. And if soldiers take away your money, don't say I never warned you. You may now go.'

We hastened away, after heaping compliments on the law enforcers who had turned against their own law and conspired with us, the law breakers.

On our return journey, we could not feel any hunger. Our pockets bubbled with notes, while bliss rose from the seat of our hearts and spread to each tissue of our bodies. After crossing the border swamp, we met our friends on the very spot we had left them. Like us the good men were also smiling, presumably as I thought, congratulating us upon our luck. I opened my mouth to thank the benevolent army men, but words were not destined to form. In a dream-like fashion both men pointed their weapons at us, and cocked them ready to fire.

'Empty your pockets, and put the money on the ground!' the first soldier barked at us.

'And be quick, did you imagine it is you we shall eat?' the second soldier yelled.

After robbing us clean, the men bade us a very kind farewell, and started heaping our money into a mound.

Up to now when I recall the incident, I vividly see us hours later, having arrived in our village, narrating the whole drama to a bow-headed Hanja. I also seem to re-experience the ache in my tired back and legs.

23
Massacre
JWL

One early morning of June 17th 1983, I was awakened by other boys who sleep with me in the same hut in the village called Natumkasikou, a surburb of Moroto town. I heard the sound of gunshots all over the town. To our surprise we heard someone knocking on our door speaking Kiswahili in an Acholi accent saying '*Nyinyi sasa mutoke inje anguka*'. We started dressing ourselves but yet bullets were being shot into the house; the door was kicked and it opened.

To my surprise as I was rushing outside, a bullet was shot at me when my head appeared out first at an angle and it nearly removed my forehead. A great miss. I fell down unconscious. The scar on my forehead will never let me forget the Acholi. It seems I was pulled away and beaten severely with kicks and flogged. Out of the six of us who were sleeping in the same hut, four were killed, namely Ngorok, Lonya, Arukol and Lochoge. Ibale was injured badly and the hut was burnt to ashes with the dead inside. My uncle, Antonio Lokwag, who was coming to the rescue was ordered to sit down and his hands were tied backwards. The rest of the people were ordered out of their huts and ordered to sit down under the tree, men were to lie upside down on their stomachs and not to look at anything with their faces downwards.

The village was severely looted; everything including record players, plates, saucepans, clothes, radios, in fact even decorated nice drinking water pots. Men with no shirts on their chests were told to stand up and make one line and start moving towards the town and to the Boma ground. Then, after a long time when I returned back to my senses, I found a lot of smoke in the village. Most huts were burnt, most people killed, including the village's famous Akongo player, Iramar Akomo and the wife of Lorogoi the meat seller called Alice Nalem and her three children inside their hut. Chicken, goats, sheep, turkeys were all taken by soldiers.

At the Boma ground, men were being sorted: those with traditional marks on their bodies, arms and faces were considered killers and were taken to the quarter guard. Others were beaten and told to produce graduated tax tickets although the majority did not produce due to being hurried outside at a wrong hour; others with only underwear, others sheets only, women in only petticoats or vitenge and children completely naked. Those led to the barracks included my uncle with his hands tied backwards but due to heavy beating, he could not walk any longer. When they were approaching the quarter guard, there is a deep valley called Kadokochin in which he was thrown down and landed on the stones; then the soldiers got a very big stone on the surface and dropped it on him and his head got broken and the brain out.

Among those I knew killed included the following: Lokut John, Engwrakachol, Kale, Apalobok, Apaliba, Lopeyon Ekonikamar, Lochugae, Longolekial Adisababa, Nangole, Konikau, Lotura, Lokathan, Yale, Lotimong, Keyian, Kalikal, Kiyonga Changana, Baidhapus, Ebokoyia, Amaikoni Lookit and his sons Aremann and Lomonyang, Achia, Lobaaluk, Lopetoron, Loonu, Lomongin, to mention but a few. Those soldiers who had never killed people could come and borrow at night from the guard and they would be allowed to come and choose the most healthy ones –like goats you want to kill for your visitors – and take and kill from the bush. The survivors of these included, Lookit, Lokut John and Achia, who were rescued.

After a week, the authorities of Moroto district arose and went to inspect the army cells and only got three people with bad big wounds of knife cuts on almost all parts of the body. Thus, out of the eighty or more people only three survived. In fact when the scene of murder was reached by the Bishops of the Church of Uganda, Right Rev. Davis Howell and his clergy, Bishop representative of the Catholic church Fr Joseph Garavello, popularly known as Apalokoni, heads of departments, R.Cs, they found a lot of bodies which had been scattered by vultures, hyenas, crows and kites. One would see that as if it was the valley of dry bones as Prophet Ezekiel was shown in his vision.

No steps were taken against these unbelievable atrocities against humanity, since the army was the overall power. Everybody was afraid for his or her life. This was reported to Obote, but nothing was done to these Commanders of Moroto Military barracks. At one time, on 29th July, 1983 the army, after losing a match to the police 3-0, fought an armed battle and four police constables were killed, and so many civilians again suffered the fate of being killed and injured.

After two months when I recovered from hospital, I was brought home slowly. I gained back my condition as normal. Then on the 2nd November 1983, one late afternoon we were shooting birds behind Moroto Municipal school. I saw a soldier coming tactfully carrying a military bag. The rest of the boys ran away and disappeared in the school garden. As for me, I hid by the thorn bushes. I saw a warrior coming towards the soldier and the soldier gave the warrior the bag and then the warrior gave the soldier a very big block of money, and they separated.

As the warrior was going westwards following the valley, slowly, I followed him. He hid the bag and he proceeded to Acholi Inn to drink, waiting for darkness to come and collect his bag. When he disappeared I removed the bag and hid it in a very thick bush and I went home. The next day I came to check what was in the bag. Oh-oh! A lot of bullets! I also kept quiet.

On the 14th November 1983, my mother was roasting flour for local brew and this is when I saw one of the firewood burning but the smoke came out of the end point like an exhaust pipe. I got interested in this wood and extinguished the fire. When I examined it, it had a big pith but within the inter-nodes it was like a bamboo and worms had made holes from inter-node to inter-node. I removed it and tried to put one bullet in the pith using a knife to open the inter-nodes carefully; and the bullet fitted well.

On the 17th of the same month I stole my mother's 150 shillings and bought only that type of firewood from a woman called Irega from Rupa. I and a child of my late uncle called Tychicus took the firewood to the scene of the bag and with our knives fitted all the 300 bullets inside the firewood. On the 18th, it had rained the previous night and the roads were muddy, the morning was very cold and no charcoal or firewood sellers were around. So, we decided to sell our firewood to the army when their TATA truck came looking for firewood for cooking. We sold at 22 shillings only and used the money to eat pancakes (Kabalagala).

The soldiers after buying what was enough for the day, took and used the firewood. It seemed at the time they were serving porridge and that was when the deadly fire reached the firewood. Bullets exploded and 27 soldiers died instantly, three of their cooks and their cooking utensils were completely destroyed and nobody up to now knows where the bullets came from and who did it. I thank God for the wisdom he gives to his people who are oppressed by the unruly people. I made a compensation for their dead and their families through God's inspiration. This was the worst I have ever seen in my life in Uganda.

24
Terror on the Road
Masyale Sowedi Wayenga

At the junction where the roadblock was staged, there were six long queues: two on each of the roads from Iganga, Tororo and Tirinyi.

War! The country was soaked in war, and the men were battling it out who would be boss next? Kampala was already on fire, and Makerere, which had been our sole solace, had also been hit. Boom! Boom! The language of *saba-saba* was well known to everyone. Amin's government was crumbling as the TPDF advanced towards Kampala.

Now I was on the road trying to reach home in the eastern part of the country. But was I really going to reach home, I wondered. I had left Lumumba Hall, Makerere University with two colleagues, Sam and Ben. But at a roadblock in Mukono, Sam had been ordered to sit down. No what, no why, simply to sit down at the side of the road, and that was the last I saw of him. Ben, even Ben was not lucky enough to cross the Nile at Jinja.

The roadblocks! Oh, those roadblocks.

Right now my heart was in my mouth. Was I really going to go over this one?

Nakalama! This Nakalama one? Only Allah knew!

My feet shook a little, and I laboured to control my breathing. All the veins around me pulsed with fatigue. For a good four days I had barely eaten or slept. I was on the brink of collapsing.

My queue, which was on the left of the road from Iganga, was bound for Tirinyi while the one on the right, directly opposite us, was for Tororo. The same applied to the road from Tororo. The queue on the right was people going to Iganga, while the one on the left was for those bound for Tirinyi. And from Tirinyi, the queue on the left, directly facing us, was for Iganga, while the one on the right was for Tororo.

From this or the other road, however, our destiny was all determined at the junction itself. Whoever was found innocent stepped into the middle of his or her road at the centre of the junction. The junction did not have a roundabout, but only a corner to Tirinyi.

Anyhow, I was still very far from that centre and could not determine, in specific terms, what was going on there. All I knew was that they were checking for culprits and guerrillas!

We stood in the water-passage at the side of the road each glued to his or her position. Only occasionally, when someone was freed at the junction, did we move an inch or so.

A few people could be seen trickling along the tarmac road, those who had been freed from Tororo and Tirinyi roads and were heading for Iganga. But even these walked in single file. Elderly men and women walked with their heads heavily bowed down.

Ours, too. Incidentally, even ours! Because at this roadblock one looked up only at his or her own risk. If a response was required from you, then you gave it to the boss while either looking down or at your shoulder, depending on where that boss was standing. The law! The unbreakable law!

And so those freed continued to pass us. Almost like ghosts!

As I observed, an absent-minded walker stepped in one of the holes, tumbled and almost fell. She quickly pulled herself together and continued walking. She was very lucky: they had not seen her. She was extremely lucky she had not fallen. Because she would have broken another law. Noise! To make noise at the roadblock!

Business! Mind your own business, I told myself as I turned my eyes to where I was supposed to look: between my legs. I saw my trousers. I saw my shoes. Oh, the damn trousers had originally been grey. The damn shoes had originally been black.

Shoes, trousers, oh don't mind all these damn things, but the grass I was standing on. The grass had been scorched dry. Scorched totally, by not only the constant trampling on by people's feet, but also by the searing sun. The period of the year was November, and as we squeezed ourselves in the single file, the sunlight sent down powerful rays on to us, making us sweat through and through. It added to the intensity of the situation: the irascible soldiers, the guns hanging dangerously from their shoulders, the silence, the tarmac road, then now this tremendous heat from the sun! Hell! This was simply hell on earth!

I found myself getting nearer to the junction. Four soldiers had been walking near our queue from one end of it to the other. The same was happening to the other queues as well. But up to now I had not established what exactly they were looking for. As they walked at the zig-zag edges of the road, they only occasionally stopped at places where women or girls stood. My zone in the queue did not have any woman or girl, so I was totally green about their whole intention, especially on the two queues for Tororo. Maybe later I would discover, I did not know.

On, on we shuffled our feet till I was now only two people to reach the target. I could see the people whose fate was also about to be determined very clearly on all the roads. Between my queue and that one from Tirinyi, just beside there on the left, I could also see a hut hurriedly made out of sticks and grass. It was fairly big and its inside was sheltered off with canvas. However, seated on its left verandah, and stretching right from inside, was a line of beautiful girls. There existed two similar huts for the other queues, and oh, I could now see why the four soldiers had been walking along each queue. To extract these jewels for the bigger bosses. That had been their assignment.

The beautiful queens! Oh, those beautiful queens! Their heads, as usual, were heavily bowed, and they were sobbing. Sobbing not openly but from their hearts.

Of course, nobody was supposed to look at them, and if found, found!

But as human beings we, all the same, managed to steal looks at them.

Then on the right of the hut: what a sharp contrast! This one was occupied by 'guerrillas'! Men, young and old, who had not satisfactorily met the requirements of the roadblock. 'Guerrillas'! Yes, 'proven guerrillas' who had all along, in one way or another, tried to topple the regime. Their shirts had been stripped off, and they sat there half-naked; sweat profusely running down their faces and entire bodies. For those who were hairy, beads of the sweat could be seen locked within the hair on their chests.

I could now feel the real heaviness of the roadblock. For those 'guerrillas' anything could happen to them any moment. Even me who was still in the queue could become a guerrilla any moment. Then anything could also happen to me at that moment!

Death. The atmosphere was getting more and more charged with death!

There were now two people I was most interested in: the young man right in front of me and the soldier, the boss, who was checking our queue. I had not had any chance to look at the young man's face. But from his youthful neck, I could indeed tell he was not quite old. To the level of senior two or, maximumly, a senior three fellow.

A sheet of pimples evenly spread on the French-cut he had made on his head. Those at the bottom of the neck were bigger, while upwards, they thinned out graphically into the thicker hair, almost proudly. The big shoes he was in and the generally exaggerated attire he had adorned himself in all pointed to his youthfulness.

Then the soldier! The boss! Yes, the boss! I could not, of course, look at him as freely and as much as I wanted. But there he was towering over all of us. Tall Thick! Enormous! Twala, the king of the Kuikuanas!

He stood directly facing Tirinyi Road, and so I could steal looks at only one side of his face. The nose stood on his face like an unburned brick and the scars, oh yes, the scars these were as deep as the groove on a circumcised penis. Sweat running down them. Then the lips, these were thick, thick like the hind of a cow about to deliver. The upper one burdened more with a head-like creation on its middle top.

I had heard that in democratic systems the leaders requested, if not almost begged, their subjects: 'Vote for me. Please, vote for me. I'll build you a school there, one hospital there and a road over there.' However, if right now this Master shouted at us, 'I will be your Master forever! I will be your Boss forever and ever', we would have immediately answered back, 'Yes, Sir! 'Yes, Sir, forever and ever!'

I stood at attention. The sensation that I was any moment going to face this man quickly engulfed my entire being. Pu! Pu! I could hear the heart beating inside me Then it happened!

'Iyo nini? Iyo nini?' The soldier checking the queue from Tirinyi going to Tororo was shouting. He was checking an elderly man wearing a dirty brown kanzu and an old torn coat.

We all turned our attention there. Momentarily, everything else stopped at the roadblock. The soldier was pointing with his gun at a swollen thing in the old man's kanzu. It looked like a ball between his legs.

'Ugonjwa,' quickly replied the old man, now thoroughly shaken up.

'Apana!' roared again the soldier. *'Ugonjwa gani uwo?!'*

That could never be sickness! He was not prepared to be taken by surprise. He had seen, he had had enough of those surprises. That must be a bomb!

'Aya towa nguo zako zote! Juu! Haraka!' he thundered.

The old man did not lose a second. He immediately pulled up his kanzu, right up, exposing a huge, round hydro-cell! *Empanama!* Yes, the famous *empanama.* 'We all looked'. The short shrunken penis standing timidly on its top' standing right there like a blunt arrow, its skin shyly smiling off the mouth it was supposed to cover.

Funny! Very funny indeed, but there we were, completely mum. Even the soldier himself was slightly confused as to what to do next. Then the young man, right in front of me, burst out in laughter . Long, long, uncontrolled laughter. Everybody again turned to see. Who was this courageously daring person who had broken the 'law'.

Our boss immediately threw away his identity card and all the other papers he was checking and slapped him right in the middle of his face. The young man staggered and almost fell.

Towa sati yako! He thundered at him, his wildness almost twice the first one's.

Outrightly, this young man had not only broken the 'law' of keeping silence, total silence, at the roadblock, but also of interfering in the internal affairs of other queues!

No joking! If he had not all along realised and imbibed the real gravity at the road block, now he did. He complied immediately, throwing away his heavy blue sweater, and the white yellow-flowered shirt that had been inside.

'Lala chini!! Aya, lala chini!! Kwamugongo!! Mara moja!' Judging from the circumstances, the emphasis was just unnecessary.

The young man, probably also imagining he would be pardoned, again immediately laid on his back. Laid straight, just beside the other 'guerrillas' seated near the hut.

What we saw! Then what we saw! The soldier opened the knife at the mouth of his gun and, in a flash, drove it into the upper part of the young man's stomach. With equal force, he then pulled it downwards, up to the navel, and oh, intestines! Blood! Rivers of blood were now flowing everywhere! Terror! Terror was now everywhere on the road.

The young man kicked his legs violently, till as life continued to flow out of him the kicks became less and less violent. He thrust his hands once in the air, and as he put them down everything came to a total stand still.

The soldier folded his knife, wiped the blood on his fingers onto his trousers and came back to the queue. Just like that, and I was the next person to be checked. Whether I was alive, half-alive or something else I just couldn't tell. I simply vaguely saw him come back to his position.

Well, I had in any case, already prepared myself for this moment. Before anything else, you had to know the language of the roadblock. Partly it was this language that had enabled me to go through the other roadblocks at Mukono and Jinja. But would that trick also really bear fruits here? Suppose, just suppose the quid I had folded and put in the identity card was not enough for this Boss? What would happen? Moreover, this was all I now had. What would really happen?

He extended his bloody hand for the identity card. He got out the money without any ado and put it in his pocket. He did not even count it.

Good. This was good luck. Probably all would be OK for me.

I looked completely down as he fixed his gaze on the identity card. From the way he held it, however, I could see it was upside down. When held in normal position LUMUMBA HALL was on top while MAKERERE UNIVERSITY was at the bottom. But now it was the reverse.

Before he asked me anything, he took some time nodding his head. He was absorbed in total concentration. Eventually he got out the word, and asked me, this time not in Swahili but in English. 'Why go Makerere?' As usual it was with a lot of force.

What a question! I had to think very fast. Any moment now, any slight mistake now and I would also be like the young man lying in the pool of blood, and on whom little black ants had already started to climb.

'I go there; I called there,' I replied slowly, adopting his mode of English.

But then amidst the tense atmosphere, I forgot and also looked at him. A mistake! What a big mistake, directly looking at the boss! The law! I had broken the law!

Two things had messed up my fortune!

'I? I?' he shouted back at me. He was pointing at himself, 'I go Makerere?!' He was totally enraged. What? When? How? Where? Words! Enough for words! The next thing I received was also a slap right in the middle of my face. Like a young man, I staggered and almost fell. I ended up near the 'guerrillas' at the hut, the dead body slightly to the right. And as he got ready to...

Noise! Noise! There was too much noise at the roadblock! Why? What was happening? Were the boys failing to properly conduct the exercise?

This forced the big boss, or one of them, to come out of the hut. I did not know how many they were, and what they were exactly doing inside there.

In appearance he was no better than the boss who had almost shot me, except that he was shorter.

'Nini?' he asked, after pressing his trousers upwards and holding himself akimbo. *'Kerere, nasikiya kerere mingi sana, kwanini?'*

My would-be assailant relaxed his gun and saluted him. He again preferred to respond in English.

'First one break law.' He pointed at the dead young man. 'He make noise here. I dealt him ready! Him ready! Second now Makerere! He asked me a question! He know much!'

He did not mention the *empanama* man from whom all this chaos had started. I squeezed my teary eyes and peered at the queue where he had been, hoping to see him. But he was not there. Probably he had been freed and left for home.

'OK. OK,' replied the big boss. 'I have understand. But two cases all come where?'

'Here, here Afande,' the other replied a bit excitely. The big boss should know he was doing the right thing at the roadblock.

'OK, OK, I seen. They are people fight us! Think this Tanzania! Discipline *yote!* Twenty *Kiboko! Kila mtu! Wale wa nine iko wapi?*'

The four soldiers who had been walking along our queue rushed to the scene and saluted.

'Aya, ishirini kwa kila mumoja!' The Big Boss directed. 'That one cry, add more! Now! I want see!'

Even without being told to lie down, the entire queue was already flat on their stomachs. Right flat on the spoilt tarmac, and the soldiers were at work with the leather belts they had unfastened from their waists. *Kwa! Kwa!* Everywhere was now kwa! Kwa! With kiboko. Terror, everywhere along the queue was now only terror.

Saba-Saba. Oh, when was *saba-saba* going to reach here? Boom! only one Boom! would scatter these terrorists, would annihilate all of them!

Cry, no cry, but all the same some people broke the law!

The order! Especially the women, boys and girls. As the kiboko cut more and more into them, urine could also be seen freely running down the tarmac where they lay.

Up to now I had only been standing there, watching. But without taking notice the big boss charged at me with something in his right hand. It was a metallic whip. I believe he wanted to restore order and calmness at the roadblock before he could retire again to the hut. So he decided to deal with me, the 'ring-leader', himself. The other 'ring-leader' had already been finished!

The pain of the whip sent me flying in the air. Flying, flying till I found my level just beside the dead body. Right flat on my torso.

The big boss quickly put aside the whip. It was probably wasting his time, and pulled a knife from his pocket and jabbed me with it. Madly jabbed me on the back. I counted five good bouts in different places till now my entire body was paralysed with pain.

I instinctively rolled over, and one of my hands fell on his right shoe. He appeared to be impatient. Two forces must have been driving him now. To demonstrate to his juniors that there were many tactics of finishing off a guerrilla of my type, or simply the desire to go back to the hut.

So now he shifted to kicking. I had inspired his leg by touching it.

Kicked! He kicked me right on the head! Kicked! Till now, oh, the shoe caught my right eyebrow! God! God! The entire eye was now right out there! I could feel the hot blood running down my cheek.

The big boss could have probably been excited, or even amused, by the sight of the eye. It must have looked like a tennis ball. So he decided to kick it back into its socket.

He kicked once: it did not go! Twice: it did not go! Why? Was this eye also stubborn like its owner?

He now stepped on it once with all his force, and it burst, splashing its contents in all directions. Oh, the pain. Now the pain. Oh, Oh.

I again instinctively raised the upper part of my body, waved my arms in the air and fell right across the dead young man.

That was all! All I now very faintly heard from the big boss was: 'Now finish! Continue work!'

I must have slept beyond midnight, probably beyond even 2.00 am. Then I seemed to hear some voices, faint, very faint voices: 'Where did they leave the bodies? Where could they have left them?

I could not move. I could not feel any part of my body. I could not even tell where I was or, for that matter, tell even what had happened to me. But I was alive. Yes, I knew I was still alive.

The sounds grew louder, slightly louder, and from what was being said and how it was being said, I could tell these were not army men. They were, moreover, talking in Lusoga. Some little sense was coming back to me. However, I continued lying across what appeared to be a few feet of sponge mattress.

Anyhow, the searchers eventually reached us and quickly lifted me and put me aside, intending to leave me there. But to their biggest surprise, I slowly lifted my legs and sat up!

The rest was narrated to me later.

The roadblock had stopped at 7.00 pm sharp, as it normally did. Word had gone round that two people had been murdered at Nakalama. One a young man called Gideon Waiswa from Busembatia, and the other a student from Makerere University hailing from Bugwere.

Busembatia being relatively near Nakalama, the relatives of Gideon decided to collect him that very night. Braving the darkness and all the risks involved, they used *panya* routes till they reached the place. They were five in number and three of them had bicycles.

They could not leave me behind. They now just couldn't leave me behind. The Basoga are our distant relatives and above all, they are human beings. But, on the other hand, I had also proved a nice shock to them. Instead of finding me dead as it had been communicated to them, I was alive! Still alive!

However, luckiest of all, was the fact that the Basoga had come with an extra bicycle. Under severe pain, I sat on that bicycle till we reached Busembatia. I spent the rest of that night in Busembatia Dispensary. No time was wasted. The following day my friends delivered me to Pallisa Hospital where I recovered slowly, slowly till I went back home.

Peace! Now we have some peace in this country. But when I see some people again trying to jeorpadise that hard-won peace, especially those who forget so quickly and those who seek for themselves, I simply shudder. Who knew I would now be a one-eyed man? I simply refer them to the Kigwere proverb; *'Atamaite ekiita akanamira musyo'*. He who does not know what kills, exposes his nakedness to fire. Some Ugandans have really physically suffered while some have only heard about that suffering.